A Passage through Sacred History

A Passage through Sacred History

&

Lenten Reflections for Individuals and Groups

Don C. Skinner

United Church Press Cleveland, Ohio

United Church Press, Cleveland, Ohio 44115
© 1997 by United Church Press

Excerpt from Joan Clifford Hutter, *The Chautauquan Daily,* 4 July 1996 editorial, used by permission of the author. Excerpt from James Weldon Johnson, "The Creation," in *God's Trombones: Seven Negro Sermons in Verse* (New York: Viking, 1927), used by permission of the publisher.

Biblical quotations are from the New Revised Standard Version of the Bible, © 1989 by the Division of Christian Education of the National Council of the Churches of Christ in the U.S.A., and are used by permission

All rights reserved. Published 1997

Printed in the United States of America on acid-free paper

02 01 00 99 98 97 5 4 3 2 1

Library of Congress Cataloging-in-Publication Data

Skinner, Don C., 1932–
A passage through sacred history : Lenten reflections for individuals and groups / Don C. Skinner.
p. cm.
ISBN 0-8298-1216-4 (pbk. : alk. paper)
1. Lent—Meditations. 2. Bible—History of Biblical events.
I. Title.
BV85.S57 1997
242' .34—dc21 97-33603
CIP

Contents

Introduction

Grace and peace to you from the Creator who gives us being, the Incarnate Word who gives us hope, and the Holy Spirit who gives us courage.

This book is not an inclusive guide to biblical faith. The "footprints" it explores are but a few among many that might have been chosen. And even those few receive sketchy treatment.

So why write the book!? To assist Christian congregations in three ways:

1. By highlighting some key events in the complex procession we call "sacred history," through which twentieth-century Christians find their roots in the faith of the ancient Hebrews.

2. By stimulating lively and thoughtful discussion among those Christians as a Lenten discipline. (The seven-chapter format is designed to facilitate a seven-week Lenten study/discussion experience.)
3. By helping those Christians to arrive at Easter better equipped to understand what they are doing there!

The author recommends that those using this book, whether individually or as part of a group, have at hand a Bible (preferably the New Revised Standard Version, since quotes in the text are drawn from it) and a pad and pencil. Jotting down questions and observations as they occur will facilitate both individual learning and group discussion.

The author also encourages those who will discuss the book as a group to individually pray for one another before starting to read each chapter. By focusing your spiritual energy in this manner, you will insure that your time together is profitable, whether you get anything out of the book or not!

1

The Promise

All glory comes from daring to begin.

—Anonymous

We Christians have a distinct advantage. We are able to view the entire biblical drama after the fact. Theologians say we have a "post-Resurrection faith," that is, we look back at the life of Jesus from the perspective of people who have already read the last chapter and know how the book ends. But not just the Jesus story. We look at the whole biblical saga that way. Not that there is anything wrong with that. We could hardly do otherwise. We live at the end of the story, at least as far as the story has unfolded to date—a theme we'll revisit in chapter 7. But if we are not careful, this vantage point influences the way we think about Scripture and the people who inhabit it and becomes an interpretive trap. Let me illustrate.

Can you think of moments in your life when you were scared out of your wits? Maybe the doctor found something troubling in a routine lab test. Or you were driving down the highway minding your business when something happened for which you were totally unprepared and you thought—just for an instant—that you might be killed. Or a momentous incident occurred suggesting that we might be about to lose control as a nation—a Cuban missile crisis or an Oklahoma City bombing. Or a frightful natural event, such as an earthquake or tornado, threatened your family.

I remember such an episode. My family had been camping in northern Minnesota and we were driving back to St. Paul on a two-lane state highway, enjoying what weather forecasters like to call "unsettled weather." Indeed. With no warning, the sky darkened and a massive curl of black cloud, five hundred feet aloft, rolled over us from the west like a gigantic breaker poised to tumble onto an ocean beach. Have you ever crossed the prairies of America's upper midwest? The only shelter you're likely to find out there is your hat. There was no place to hide. As the cloud rolled over us, a burst of wind slammed into our van so hard that we were instantly thrown into the opposing traffic lane. Fortunately, no one was in it! Simultaneously, rain and hail struck the van's metal skin, not from above, but from the side, creating such a din that we could communicate only by shouting. I looked over to see my ten-year-old son, in the passenger seat, tugging at his tightly closed and locked door as if it was about to fly away: water bubbled in around its edge like froth around the lid of a boiling pot. I remember asking myself one of those questions that makes sense at the moment, but later seems totally absurd: "What do you do with the steering wheel and brake pedal when your car leaves the ground?"

If you can think of such an incident, think back on it now. How did you feel when right in the middle of it? Did you ignore it as a momentary bother, glibly reassuring yourself that everything would turn out fine? Or were you scared out of your wits?

Now, consider: if you suddenly had the power, in the middle of that incident, to know that everything would indeed turn out okay, how would your response have changed? How would your *feelings* have differed? It would be more like having a tooth drilled or receiving an injection. Not the kind of thing we line up for in eager anticipation. But we know it will be over soon and we will be better for it. But when you've lost control of the vehicle in which your family is riding and you have reason to believe that a tornado just might be churning the prairie twenty yards to starboard, you have no such reassurance! For all you know, you'll be dead in a few seconds. Which is why feelings are so intense at such a moment. The unknown and unknowable focus our emotions superbly!

How easily we forget this human reality when we read Scripture. Events that would rouse the most intense emotion were we personally involved—*and if we didn't know the outcome ahead of time*—are read with all the exhilaration of attending a PTA meeting. "Ho hum, here's Elijah up against 450 prophets of Ba'al, but he's going to win, so it's okay. Score another one for the good guys." It's all so easy.

Self-respecting Christians should view this state of affairs with alarm, because we are a people whose identity and purpose is shaped by story. We view ourselves through the story of a faith community. Our understanding of the transcendent, of the "why" of the universe, of human nature and destiny, take shape through story. But if, in reciting and receiving these stories, we filter out the depth of emotion endured by the oh-so-very-human folk who people them, we reduce their lives to a Bible trivia quiz. What is more, we degrade our own story. After all, if what they experienced was as flat as our telling of it often suggests, what self-respecting pilgrim of faith would follow them? And what does that say about *us*?

Dr. Martin Luther King Jr. used to refer to a man for whom recent physicial death merely confirmed the death of the spirit years previously. And an Episcopal priest once lamented the tedium of conducting Christian funeral services because, when he entered the church, he wasn't always sure which end of the room held the body. Both appeared to be equally dead!

What had been lost that caused two devoted clergy to talk this way? The life-giving power of story, our story, a *good* story. In fact, its value can hardly be overstated.

This is the task I propose for us during this Lenten period: to discover—or rediscover, as the case may be—the feeling-full quality, the aliveness, of the biblical story. We will do it by touching on seven moments in biblical history, moments that may usefully be thought of as "footprints in our passage through sacred history." They are stories that demonstrate God's gifts to, and claim on, humanity. If we can do this, we will come to Easter with a vitality that many of us only dimly comprehend and some of us have lost entirely. For as the story lives for us, we come alive for the story.

We begin with a man and woman who, though barely accessible to us across the abyss of time, took the first step of what has become our faith journey. Their original names were Abram and Sarai, and they are said to have originated in a place with a poetic name: Ur of the Chaldeans (Genesis 11:27–31). At the time, Ur was a Sumerian city in the lower Euphrates River valley. We know it as the part of Iraq that lies nearest Kuwait, the invasion of which brought on what Americans now call the Gulf War, or Desert Storm. It would be difficult to imagine anyone less like us, living a daily life more different from ours. They were nomads, living in tents similar to those used by the Bedouins who still roam the Near East. By our standards, they owned little. Their primary mode of transport was their feet. They survived mainly by herding animals. We would view their diet as limited.

Biblical scholars are uncertain about a number of things concerning Abram and Sarai, not least being how we ought to consider them. Are we to understand them to have been discrete persons or as the symbolic antecedents of the Hebrew nation? For us, the more significant question may be: Does it make any difference? For whether Abram and Sarai lived as individual human beings or represent a folk ancestry is really unimportant. What is important is what they embody at the onset of Hebrew religious awakening: they are the vehicle of The Promise. And taking that promise seriously required one large dose of faith.

Consider the story. In company with his father Terah, Abram, Sarai, and Abram's nephew Lot left Ur and walked (!) 550 miles northwest to Haran (near the modern border of northern Iraq and Syria). They settled there for a time, during which Terah died and was buried. Then occurred one of the seminal events of biblical history, to which Abram's response earned his place in history. God spoke to him.

Imagine: you are relaxing in your back yard one afternoon, thinking about firing up the barbecue, when you hear a voice. It may sound only in the recesses of your mind. You may be the only one who hears it. That's not important. The voice is real. And it addresses *you*. "Pack up your household, say farewell to your friends and relatives, and move to a land that I'll show you when you get there. I'll give you so many offspring you won't be able to count them; and because of you, every nation of earth will consider itself blessed." What kind of an order is that? How would you respond? A lot of people I know would add, "And if you buy that one, I own a nifty bridge in Brooklyn I'd like to discuss with you." I suspect that at best I'd be a tad reluctant, at worst terrified! But you really should pause a moment here and read the *real* version, at Genesis 12:1–3; but remember: read for feeling, not just narrative.

The most remarkable part of the story is not that God spoke. God conversed with people all through the Bible. The remarkable thing is that Abram and Sarai, in spite of the feelings they surely must have had, got up and went. They swallowed hard, called together the people of their household, packed their tents, corralled their animals and started down the road to some place the location of which they did not know and wouldn't recognize when they got there—all as an act of faith.

Which raises a priority question: what *is* faith?

To answer it, I must first invite you on a short side trip, to consider what faith is not. That may sound silly. But it can be demonstrated that most of us use our Christian vocabulary more by habit than insight. We really *don't* always know what the words mean. First, suppose someone asked, "Do you believe the sun will rise tomorrow?" and you replied, "Yes," would that be a faith statement? No. It is an acknowledgment of the consistency of natural law. The sun always comes up in the morning—at least consistently enough that human beings feel comfortable with "always." (Well, mostly. I live in Oregon, and there are days!)

Suppose a friend asked, "Do you believe God exists?" Would your "yes" be a confession of faith? Most people would say so. They'd be wrong. Faith is not agreement with an intellectual proposition. That is, faith is not the same as belief. And while "Does God exist?" remains a popular topic of debate, from a biblical viewpoint the question is meaningless. The *existence* of God is not thought worthy of discussion. To say with the psalmist "Fools say in their hearts, 'There is no God'" (Psalm 14) is not to argue the existence of God, but to challenge those who believe they can treat the poor with contempt and get away with it because no one sees. God sees, the psalmist declares, and will score their depravity with abject terror.

Then what is faith? What do we mean when we say we "have faith" if not that we believe in the existence of God? Imagine a world where food and water are scarce. Drought dogs your steps and famine hovers at your campfire. There is only marginal certainty that food and drink will be there when your family needs them. Failure of the winter rains is a death sentence. It is a world in which tribal affinities are absolute, tribal conflict a daily possibility. In which the birth of a child is an event of monumental significance, because it promises that your people continue to have a grip on existence. In which every geologic and topographical feature may hide a capricious spirit with the potential—perhaps the intent—to do evil.

In such a world, God told Abram and Sarai to pack up and start traveling. Why on earth (or should we phrase that, why for heaven's sake) did they *do* it? *Hesed,* that's why. Come again, you ask? *Hesed* holds the answer. It is a Hebrew word for which there is no ready equivalent in English. The best interpretation is "radical faithfulness." Whatever else we may say about God, this much is certain: *God's promise may be depended upon absolutely.* No ifs, ands, or buts. God's word is good. Period.

Does it seem unnecessary to point this out? I think not. You see, Christians spend a lot of time discussing whether or not God is omnipotent (all-powerful), omniscient (all-knowing), and omnipresent (able to be everywhere at the same time). These are called the "attributes" of God, and they dominate our thinking far more than we realize. If such ideas appeal to you, and you have not already read scholastic philosophers like St. Thomas Aquinas, you may want to do so. But for our purpose here, it is necessary to point out that the Hebrews—in this case Abram and Sarai—would consider the whole discussion a waste of time.

Why? Because they were not concerned with God's attributes, but with God's *character.* After all, God is God. All powerful? Unquestionably. All knowing? Without doubt. Always present? I surely hope so! But none of that matters. What matters is, *can God be trusted?*

The Hebrew's "yes" to that question is at the heart of their vision of God. You can place absolute trust in divine promises. Think of living in Sarai and Abram's world. If a petulant, capricious deity is in control, how can you survive? It would be wiser to find the highest cliff in the neighborhood and jump off. Because if holiness—with all its power over life—cannot be trusted, life becomes intolerable. Better to be dead. History brims with stories of societies that threw maidens into fuming volcanoes, cut children's throats (on which more below!), or engaged in equally detestable practices in order to propitiate some cosmic adolescent.

It was this utter confidence in the faithfulness of a loving God that moved Abram and Sarai to pack up and go. God made a promise—three of them, actually: a homeland, offspring beyond counting, and a blessing for humanity. Perceiving that promise to be utterly devoid of equivocation, Sarai and Abram trusted and walked. And that is the proper definition of faith: *utter trust in God's faithfulness to promises made.* When we affirm our faith in God, we testify that God is, has been, and always will be absolutely trust*worthy.*

From a biblical point of view, however, nothing comes easy. The road Abram and Sarai took at God's call held torturous twists and turns. To begin with, there was the small matter of age. This couple, as the expression has it, were a bit long in the tooth. More to the point, they were childless. True, there was Ishmael, son of Abram by Hagar, Sarai's Egyptian slave girl. But he was a surrogate heir, in keeping with an ancient custom that legitimized the offspring of a man and his barren wife's female servants. But it was not the same, and everyone knew it. Yet God called Abram out of his tent one night and said, "Look toward heaven and count the stars, if you are able to count them. So shall your descendants be" (Genesis 15:5). By what line of descendence? Where was the child—Abram and *Sarai's* child—who would wrap that promise in flesh?

Have you ever known a couple who desperately wanted children but could not conceive? Have you traced their attempts, month after month, year after year, to make real the compelling dream? Have you witnessed their surge of joy when it just might be happening? Or tasted the bitterness of their tears when, one more time among times too numerous, the hope is shattered? Imagine yourself in a culture where a woman's deepest humiliation is to be barren. Not only is she denied the joy of birthing a child; she is a laughing stock. When a woman's greatest glory is to insure the continuation of family, a barren woman is useless, a conjugal and social flop.

A sexist viewpoint? Clearly. Would we tolerate such treatment of a woman in our congregation? I hope not! But before we digress into a rash of righteous indignation and self-congratulation for superior social sensitivity, pause and consider: this was Sarai's reality, the legitimacy of which she not only accepted but affirmed by her participation. If you'd care to witness the abuse of which Sarai herself was capable, pause a moment and read two related stories in Genesis: 16:1–6 and 21:8–19.

These accounts cast Sarai in a less than flattering light, do they not? Did you find her conduct distressing? Yet we must, on reading the seamier moments in the lives of our forebears in faith, remember this central wonder of the biblical story: by means of such very imperfect human beings, God's sacred history unfolds and salvation is given. It is part of the Hebrews' genius that they hid nothing of their peoples' character. Women and men are depicted with all their warts, in all their splendid contradictions. The Apostle Paul said it best: "We have this treasure in clay jars, *so that it may be made clear that this extraordinary power belongs to God and does not come from us*" (2 Corinthians 4:7). Fragile vessels indeed. Yet Jesus himself declared that the church, though peopled by such flimsy and imperfect folk, is so mighty that hell itself is impotent to stop it (Matthew 16:18).

In spite of all this, God continues to press Abram and Sarai toward the promise, formalizing their relationship in a covenant (Genesis 17) that changes their names to Abraham ("Father of a Multitude") and Sarah ("Princess"). But Sarah remains as barren with her new name as she was with her former one.

In light of all the above, it is not difficult to understand Sarah's reaction to events at the Oaks of Mamre (see Genesis 18:9–15). Human beings possess a dazzling array of defenses against pain and disappointment. And this late in her life, Sarah was not going to give in easily to hope! In the modest language of the text, "It had ceased to be with Sarah after the manner of women." In modern clinical language, less discrete if more accurate, Sarah was post-menopausal. So much for children. Her despair was complete. Given access to what we call "the wonders of modern medicine" (code language for our refusal to let nature take its course!) Sarah's condition might not have seemed "irreversible." But to Sarah, the door was closed and bolted. What presumption, then, to have three strangers stroll up to their camp and announce that she would soon be pregnant! A psychologist friend once noted, with what I have since concluded was true insight, that anxiety is the prerequisite to humor. Human beings are not amused by the irrelevant, but by what matters. Through laughter, we diminish the burden of fear, make light of forces we cannot control, and defuse the anguish of despair. Sarah is at her most believable when she bursts into laughter at the sound of angel voices.

And then, a miracle. It is not the last time in sacred history that a child's birth will tug the promise toward fulfillment. But at what price?

We need to stay with Abraham and Sarah and their new child Isaac one moment longer. No sooner is the promise made credible than God threatens to void it. "Take your son, your only son Isaac, whom you love . . . and offer him as a burnt offering." Is this *God?* And if so, is God trustworthy after all?

Not only is Abraham commanded to end what has only just begun, he is taunted by God's language. "Your only son" is salt in the wound of his terror, for God knows as well as Abraham that this is the child of the promise, the sole means by which the inheritance of a mighty people can become manifest. "Whom you love." My God, do I need to be reminded? Burnt offering? Was a lifetime spent in faithful waiting merely to produce a sacrificial animal to appease an angry God?

Every fiber of our being shouts "No! It is not right!" Ah, friends, were Abraham and Sarah of such halting faith, who would now serve God? *Their* "no" would void the covenant with God. They would secure their child's life for a day, but lose it for eternity. And with it our own. Remember the final part of the promise? "In you, all the families of Earth will be blessed." That, dear friends, is you and me.

Thank God for human faith that mirrors divine faithfulness. Of course God had no intention of seeing Isaac's blood on the altar rocks. Certainly, one point of telling the story was to preclude, among our Hebrew forebears in faith, the practice of child sacrifice—a practice still common in Sarah and Abraham's world. But we wisely focus on the theological dimension of the story: only those able to trust God utterly, even when God means to march us into the valley of death's shadow, are suitable vessels to carry the story of salvation. For salvation as Scripture reveals it is not a burden to be hauled but a life to be lived.

Questions

1. In what way (if any) has this chapter changed how you think about Abraham and Sarah? Are you repelled by them? Drawn closer to them? Are you, a late twentieth-century American, really able to think of Abram and Sarai as forebears?

2. Could *you* do what Abram and Sarai did? What makes you think so? How prepared do you feel, as individual or congregation, to take to the road? Do you yet feel you know clearly what the road *is*? How might you find out?

3. What does it mean for the *church* to recognize that "faith" means confidence in God's trustworthiness. Does such an understanding require us to amend how we view ourselves? How we present ourselves to the community around us? How we do business?

2

Calling a Nation of Witnesses

Earth's crammed with heaven,
And every common bush afire with God;
But only he who sees takes off his shoes—
The rest sit round it and pluck blackberries.

—Elizabeth Barrett Browning

Begin by reading the story of Moses' encounter with God recorded in the book of Exodus. If you get caught up in the story—it is, after all, one of the central events of sacred history—read from Exodus 3:1 to 4:20. At the very least, read 3:1–15.

Elizabeth Browning's poetic fragment poses an interesting question: would we recognize the holy if it walked up and smacked us on the nose? Exodus 3 tells the wholly remarkable story of Moses' encounter with a bush that burned but was not consumed—a noteworthy event by any standard! But it is not at all evident that some, seeing that bush, would follow Moses and "turn aside and look at this great sight." "Oh, surely," you protest, "faced with a sight so extraordinary, we'd all stop and look." Would we?

In 1988, while driving across the country, we visited Yellowstone National Park, pausing at the Upper Geyser Basin to see Old Faithful strut its stuff. The crowd's anticipation grew as the predicted moment of eruption came and went with only a few tantalizing belches of hot water to accompany the clouds of steam. Every camera west of Chicago—including ours—was aimed at the spot when, at last, a scalding bolt of water surged into the air and gained altitude, a few feet, then ten, thirty, sixty feet into the air. So dense was the steam that we were allowed only glimpses of the geyser as it peeked out through its veil like a shy child through dotted swiss curtains.

It was a dazzling display of geologic energy, at once awesome and beguiling. The heat that drives that water originates, after all, deep in the earth where forces that beggar human imagination hold sway, scarcely constrained after several billion years. The water's odor betrays the infernal engine that drives the geosphere and lifts to the surface the sulfurous perfume of Earth's molten belly. To witness Old Faithful's towering outburst is to glimpse, if fleetingly, the fount of Creation. "Who shut in the sea with doors when it burst out of the womb?—when I made the clouds its garment?" (Job 38:8–9). The spectacle continued for four or five minutes before the geyser retreated to become, again, just another smoking hole perforating the floor of the lime-crusted basin.

But long before that, a curious thing happened. By twos and threes, at first a few, then in growing number, people began to drift away. The spectators lost interest far sooner than the geyser lost energy. We looked at each other in amazement. What was going on? Was it the malaise of a technological generation? Are we so conditioned by the frenetic hyperbole of seven-second sound bites that our attention span has regressed to that of a two-year-old? Or is it that we so seldom view natural events anymore that, when we do, we unconsciously filter them through the medium of a television tube—even when one is not there! Like the time our adolescent daughter, viewing a stunning sunset, blurted ecstatically (and innocently, I am sure), "Isn't it *beautiful*? Just like on TV!"

To read the history of Israel's pilgrimage from slave people to priestly nation and not miss the point altogether, we must understand this: God's intervention in the life of Israel is mediated through common things that, seen through eyes of faith, brim with holy meaning.

Be clear about the emphasis. Wonder, like beauty, is in the eye of the beholder. Try this parallel. To the medical staff, the birth of our child is all part of the day's work; to my wife and me, it is a miracle. Wherein is the difference? Certainly not in the biology of the event. The details of a child's passage from mother's womb to outer world are the same, whether viewed by medical professionals or gaping parents. The difference resides in the expectations that each brings to the event. This is not to slight the ministrations of physicians and nurses. There are good reasons to retain professionals to attend life's tenuous events—people able to remain emotionally detached, and respond objectively to the medical needs of mother and child in moments of crisis. But the meaning of an event is not exhausted by a description of its mechanics; nor is holiness visible to those who believe that the significance of things lies in their capacity to entertain. If we are unconscious to the sacred in daily events, those events have nothing to offer us but diversion, a sacral soap opera devoid of meaning.

Some may be distressed by this line of reasoning. It takes the fire out of what happened when Moses stepped onto the mountain of God. It suggests that those events drew their significance as much from Moses' receptivity as from God's initiative; that if Moses had been wandering about searching for his misplaced lunch, the moment might have passed, changing everything that followed. No, we protest: God's authority is not diminished by human inattention. It is irresistible. Anyone, standing where Moses stood, would see what Moses saw.

If such is your thinking, stop here, pick up your Bible and read three passages: Isaiah 42:18–25, Amos 7:1–9, and Matthew 25:31–46.

Is the point not clear? If we cannot see God in the commonalities that constitute daily life, we would not recognize Christ if he walked into the room and sat down beside us.

So with Moses. He observed a common bush, your average Middle Eastern desert shrub. That the bush is described as burning but not consumed points less to an extraordinary bush than to an extraordinary man. To burn without being consumed is biblical shorthand for the fact that this ordinary desert plant was being employed for a holy purpose. Through it, God reaches out to touch the man who will be Israel's spokesperson before Pharaoh, lead Israel out of slavery to its dread encounter with God at Sinai, bear the tablets of the Law, and represent the nation in enactment of the covenant that seals the promise made half a millennium earlier to Abram and Sarai.

Those who still doubt that Moses' spiritual receptivity was a defining factor in this encounter are referred again to Exodus 3:4 and urged to take note that God did not even speak to Moses until "God saw that [Moses] had turned aside to see." Such phrases do not appear in Scripture by accident. If the temper of God sketched by Scripture is valid (and I am not prepared to say it is not) we have to do with a God who does not demand but invites; who speaks softly of divine hope and waits for our response; whose power to compel, though exceeding the aggregate power of the universe, is constrained so as to honor our freedom to choose.

Consider: "They heard the sound of God walking in the garden at the time of the evening breeze, and the man and his wife hid themselves. . . . But God called to the man, . . . 'Where are you?'" (Genesis 3:8–9). God had to ask? Or did God choose to ask, to permit a response, even one that is an admission of guilt? (Would a coerced confession have validity?)

Again: "Now there was a great wind, so strong that it was splitting mountains . . . but God was not in the wind; and after the wind an earthquake, but God was not in the earthquake; and after the earthquake a fire, but God was not in the fire; and after the fire a sound of sheer silence. When Elijah heard it, he . . . went out and stood at the entrance of the cave. Then . . . a voice . . . said, 'What are you doing here, Elijah?'" (1 Kings 19:11b–13). Wouldn't an all-knowing God *know* what Elijah was doing there? Or does God understand that only voluntary dialogue is meaningful, words between beings who are free to engage or not?

Or again: "Then one of the seraphs flew to me, holding a live coal . . . from the altar. . . . The seraph touched my mouth with it and said, 'Now that this has touched your lips, your guilt has departed and your sin is blotted out.' Then I heard the voice of God saying, 'Whom shall I send, and who will go for us?'" (Isaiah 6:8). Couldn't God simply order Isaiah to go? Or does God seek voluntary going as having greater validity?

Note the common element in these encounters: each begins not with a command, much less a demand, but a question. Not a human question, God's question. And once the question is asked, God waits for an answer.

Why would God do this? As the One whose authority undergirds our very existence, why doesn't God just tell us what to do and save us all a lot of trouble? The answer lies in the nature of love: love can only be given, never coerced.

Before expanding on that, however, we need to pause briefly to take note of another element of this story that sheds light on divine human relationships: Moses reacted to his holy charge with something less than enthusiasm! Not once, not twice, but three times, he suggests that God may have fingered the wrong servant. He first claims to have no reputation, no credentials, no authority. "Who am I that I should go to Pharaoh and bring the Israelites out of Egypt?" (Exodus 3:11). Next he asks, "But suppose they do not believe me or listen to me?" (4:1). Then he argues, "O my God, I have never been eloquent . . . I am slow of speech and . . . tongue" (4:10). Reassured on each of these points (among a number of others!), Moses finally bleats in desperation: "O my God, please send someone else" (4:13). This exchange between a persuading God and an unwilling servant is not unique to Moses. Others—Elijah, Jonah, Jeremiah, and Ananias, to name but a few—knew the same reluctance. I, for one, am comfortable with this portrayal of Moses, because I know by heart the feeble prayer, "O my God, please send someone else!" It is a topic worthy of a book of its own!

But back to love: consider a human parallel. A young man and woman meet. The woman, though attracted to the man, bides her time and takes the measure of her feelings. The man's urgency, as often occurs in young folk of the male persuasion, rapidly escalates to something bordering on insanity. He must possess her love or die. Revealing his feeling to the woman is easy enough. Acquiring some measure of hers is a different matter. Being more reserved about hanging her heart on her sleeve, she refuses to tip her hand prematurely. It is at this point in the courtship that the man is in danger of making a critical mistake: to try, by whatever means, to force her hand. It will not, it cannot, work. The harder he pushes, the greater the likelihood he'll lose what he desires most. Pushed hard enough, the woman's trust will wither, and she will withdraw.

How this applies to the love between God and humanity was captured by James Weldon Johnson in a little book titled *God's Trombones: Seven Negro Sermons in Verse*. With disarming simplicity, the opening verse of a sermon titled "The Creation" expresses a profound, often overlooked insight about God:

> *And God stepped out on space,*
> *And he looked around and said:*
> *I'm lonely—*
> *I'll make me a world.*

God lonely? Why not? Yes, yes, I know. To be God means to be perfect in Oneself, requiring no other. But what if, as John insists, "God *is* love" (1 John 4:8, emphasis added)? Love, by definition, must have a subject, an 'other' to love. And if the quality of love with which we are here concerned is *agape*—love as God loves, love that wills, first and always, the good of the loved one—then indeed we can conceive of a cosmic affliction of loneliness, until a Creation is called into being upon which to lavish the divine self. Creation allows the God-Who-Is-Love to become the God-Who-Is-Lover.

It was to just such a relationship that God called Israel. It is not by accident that many images employed by the ancient Hebrews were drawn from the vocabulary of courtship and marriage.

Before exploring this, however, another digression is necessary, without which what follows may be needlessly clouded: God did not bring Israel out of slavery for the sake of "liberty." Such is the conventional wisdom—especially as filtered through the lens of Cecil B. DeMille. At the conclusion of the film *The Ten Commandments,* before wandering off into the desert, Moses (Charlton Heston) instructs the Israelites to bear the message of liberty to all the world. This is revisionist history, unsupported by Scripture. Why the idea might arise is clear enough: when afflicted by real oppression and the real desperation it breeds, human communities find in the Exodus story a powerful metaphor of hope. But political liberation is not the purpose of the Exodus, in God's understanding or Israel's. It is a means to an end—an end stated time and again in the text: Israel, God declares, is to be freed "so that they may worship me." (Read through the Exodus 5–12 narrative some time, noting how frequently that phrase appears.)

God did not call Israel to liberation, but to relationship, the substance of which would be forged in the crucible of Sinai's desert. God would—to use an indelicate but accurate term, "cut a covenant" with Israel. It is not a pretty phrase and the reality is less so. Some might find it distasteful, if not downright repulsive. But failing to understand its meaning to ancient Israel places us at risk of missing the theological significance both of God's covenant with Israel and of the meaning of Christ's crucifixion, toward which this Lenten journey inevitably leads us.

The covenant concept was not unique to the Hebrews, nor was the method used to enact one. It was a common Near Eastern custom, the central symbol of which sprang from an erroneous, if understandable, misconception about animal physiology. Human cultures, even scientific ones like ours, impute particular qualities or emotions to the various parts of the body. (Translating them can be very humorous, actually. Transposed into the Hebrew view of things, "I love you with all my heart" comes out, "I love you with all my liver!" To the Hebrews, the liver was the seat of emotion.) Having observed that an unrestrained effusion of blood leads to death, ancient cultures concluded that blood is the seat of life.

Now if you view the world in symbolic terms, as the Hebrews did, and you enter into an inviolable covenant, and you want that covenant sealed in the most indisputable manner, the seal of choice is blood. Your covenant will be sealed with life itself. The means for doing so (and this is where we moderns find the going a bit sticky) was to bisect one or more sacrificial animals end to end, laying the halves side by side on the ground, viscera up. If the covenant was between two persons or communities, blood from half the animal(s) was spattered on one party, that from the second half on the other, to "seal" the covenant between them. If God was a party to the covenant, blood from one half was spattered on the people, while that from the other half was splashed on a stone altar, representing the holy presence.

That we find this custom troubling or sickening is beside the point. The important thing is to recognize that sealing a covenant in this manner was of the utmost seriousness. It was binding on the parties unless annulled by common assent. In this instance, however, Israel becomes bound by a far greater obligation: its partner was no other than the Creator of the Universe, who announced that *this* covenant was eternal. And for even the most devout among us, forever is a long time!

It is further important, if we are to grasp Israel's peculiar relationship with God, to distinguish between a contract—as we conceive it in twentieth-century law—and the biblical concept of covenant. They are by no means the same. A contract is a legally binding agreement between two parties, obliging them to perform certain services for each other. If either party fails to fulfill the provisions of the contract, the other may employ the police power of the state by appealing to a court of law to enforce the contract's provisions or, failing at that, to determine what compensation the aggrieved party is entitled to receive, usually determined as a monetary value.

Now the very nature of a contract—the purpose for which it is struck—is contradictory to the concept of a covenant. Neither party to a covenant can enforce its provisions on the other. Each must, solely out of a sense of commitment, give to the other what has been promised. It is for this reason that "marriage contracts" are antithetical to Christian marriage. A couple that enters into marriage focused on what "rights" each possesses, what each is due from the other, rather than what each can do for the other, has already traveled a good way along the road toward marital failure. Only as both members of a couple strive, every day, in all aspects of their alliance, to mimic God's faithfulness (remember *hesed*?), making of themselves a gift freely and eagerly given to their partner, will a marriage possess the qualities we desire for it.

Indeed, marriage so considered (as the authors of Scripture realized) is an instructive parallel to the covenant relationship between God and Israel. I realize that this image is usually considered the other way around: traditional Christian ceremonial language draws on Christ as self-sacrificing bridegroom and the church as devoted bride to shape our thinking about marriage. It is one of the enchantments of biblical theology, however, that such metaphors often serve as fruitfully when turned end for end: we can draw on our understanding of the marriage relationship to sharpen our sense of the relationship between God and Israel. We may, for example, take note of the degree to which the self-giving of each is essential to the integrity of the partnership. Neither can, finally, force the participation of the other.

This is not to argue, however, that there are no consequences for disloyalty or betrayal. When the people fail to abide by their covenant commitment (one does not wisely accuse God of doing so!) the effect is horrendous: the very moral order upon which the nation's stability hinges is undermined, with consequences both appalling and far-reaching. We will revisit this theme in the next chapter. Before taking leave of Sinai, however, we need briefly to outline Israel's covenental responsibilities.

We already noted that Israel's Egyptian slavery did not end because of liberty but to allow Israel to travel into the wilderness to worship God. But what worship! If by that term we were expecting Moses to climb Horeb to hear God say, "I want a prelude, introit, Scripture lessons, three hymns, sermon, and benediction," we're in for a swell surprise! This God has a far richer notion of "worship" than most of us expect—including, one suspects, the Israelites! "Thus you shall say to the . . . Israelites: if you obey my voice and keep my covenant, you shall be my treasured possession out of all the peoples. Indeed, the whole earth is mine, but *you* shall be for me a priestly kingdom and a holy nation" (Exodus 19:3–6, emphasis added).

The passage requires thoughtful reading. Go back and read it again—slowly. Did you catch the implicit disclaimer in the second sentence? *Everything that is, is mine already* (read: I can choose whoever I want; but of all Earth's people, I choose *you*). Sounds real nice until the next sentence defines what being "chosen" means: you shall be a holy nation. Were you ever told, probably by someone skating on the edge of anti-Semitism, that "Jews think being 'chosen' means that they are God's favorites?" Some favoritism!

This, God asserts, shall be the path of Israel's holiness: you shall worship me and me only; you shall not make idols; you shall not use my name wrongfully; you shall keep the sabbath and honor your parents; you shall not murder, commit adultery, steal, give false testimony, or covet what is not yours. In aggregate we call these the Decalogue, or Ten Commandments. They do not, by any means, exhaust the corpus of Jewish law. Several hundred more provisions are detailed in Exodus, Leviticus, and Deuteronomy. But the starting point is plain: those who mean to represent God among the nations of Earth, to be God's nation of witnesses, to be—after Abraham and Sarah—the vessel by which the nations shall know themselves blessed, must be a people whose social relations are founded on lofty moral principle. On any other terms, holy servanthood is not possible. "Immoral" and "people of God" are contradictory terms.

Whatever else we may think of the Jews, whatever else we may think of ourselves, whatever else we may suggest that God wants of us, this much is certain: God seeks a servant people; but only those willing to struggle to become, and remain, a holy nation need apply.

Questions

1. If you are reading this book alone, reflect on how readily you see God in everyday things and events. If studying as a group, try to think of illustrations when your congregation (or members of it) saw, or failed to see, the holy in everyday things and events. Why do you think this is so?

2. What hints have you picked up from this chapter concerning the church's covenant relationship with God? Of what does it consist? (No fair peeking ahead.) What parallels are you able to draw between what you understand to be God's covenant with Israel and God's covenant with the church?

3. Now for the hard one: take an inventory of your personal moral posture. Are you content with it? What might you do to adopt moral habits that will put you even more in tune with God's expectations? If studying in a group, are you able, without becoming judgmental, to share these insights? What, if anything, do you plan to do about them? What help, if any, can you offer one another?

3

Defining Holiness

Religion is a way of walking, not a way of talking.

—William R. Inge

To begin, let's set the scene. The place is Bethel, a town in the hill country ten miles north of Jerusalem at the intersection with the east-west highway joining Jericho to the Mediterranean coast. The name is significant: from *beth,* "house," and *el,* "God," thus "House of God." Its significance for the Hebrews dates back centuries: it is the site of Jacob's ladder dream, when he camped there on his journey from Beer-Sheba to Paddan-aram, where he would be married—twice: first to Leah, then Rachel. Waking from his dream, Jacob "took the stone that he had put under his head and set it up for a pillar and poured oil on the top of it. He called that place Bethel" (Genesis 28:18–19). Further enhancing its significance, Bethel was the home of the Ark of the Covenant during part of the period between 1200 to 1000 B.C.E., when the judges ruled Israel (Judges 20:18–28).

In the late tenth century B.C.E., following the death of Solomon, the monarchy was thrown into contention when two of his many sons claimed the throne and the Jewish nation broke into two, quarrelling states. The northern kingdom, called Israel, was first ruled by Jeroboam I (931–910 B.C.E.), who made his capital at Tirzah. Cut off from the temple in Jerusalem (the capital city of Judah, the southern kingdom), Jeroboam realized that he would lose the people's loyalty if he failed to create new centers of worship. His solution was to reactivate the traditional sanctuaries at Bethel, near his southern border, and at Dan in the extreme north. Such centers were known as "high places," places of religious importance. Bethel quickly became the favorite of the monarchy and therefore took on the designation "the king's high place." However, Jeroboam erected a golden calf at each high place, in blatant disregard of the second commandment. The last time that happened, the Israelites paid for their faithlessness by spending forty years wandering the Arabic peninsula!

One other bit of information to set the stage for the discussion to follow: some years later, Jeroboam II (thirteenth monarch of the northern kingdom) still favored Bethel as the site of official religious ceremonies, the tone of which were increasingly jingoistic. Because of complex military and political events, Israel was enjoying a period of unprecedented prosperity. With enemy monarchies in disarray, Jeroboam II recaptured land lost in earlier wars and Israel regained command of the Middle Eastern trade routes over which the region's rulers routinely engaged in massive blood-letting. From their point of view, there was ample economic justification: whoever controlled the trade routes controlled a source of money and power. Problem: the mercantile wealth suddenly flooding Israel was not distributed with anything remotely resembling social equity. Established families became fabulously wealthy. Dozens of others lucky enough to ride the surge quickly came to form a new monied class. Caught in abject poverty at the bottom, the masses—whose lives had been sacrificed in one war after another, who were driven off small parcels of land so that the wealthy could create massive estates, whose plight was viewed by the wealthy as a joke—suffered without redress.

Worst of all from the viewpoint of Israel's covenant responsibility to God, the very ones who might have plead their case—the priests and professional prophets charged to nurture the nation's spiritual welfare—were very reluctant to upset the apple cart of prosperity. After all, were they not God's agents? And was it not obvious that God was pleased with Israel? How otherwise to explain the political and military advances and the burgeoning accumulation of wealth. Were these not tokens of divine pleasure? Better yet, there was no end in sight. It would take their enemies years to accumulate the resources and gather the military power necessary to again challenge Israel. In the meantime, why not make hay while the sun was shining?

Imagine, then, the mood at Bethel one bright day, perhaps in early fall. The summer crop was so plentiful that storage barns could not handle it. Excess cartloads had to be stored temporarily by piling them in the oxen parking lots. Futures prices at the Samaria grain exchange had closed higher the previous week than at any time in recent memory. And tariff revenue along the trade routes was up 17 percent. Little wonder their faces glowed, their mood was ebullient, as Israel's leading families, resplendent in new finery, gathered once again to invoke divine sanction for their egregious excess. It was just a splendid day and all was well. Well, not quite.

Enter Amos, stage right, reeking of the goats who were his daily companions, snarly hair whipping about in oily disarray, eyes smoldering like volcanos recently awakened from dormancy. Boy, was he mad! (You may want your Bible beside you for this next part, opened to the first chapter of the book of Amos.)

For a man that livid, he started out calmly enough, with pronouncements sure to please the Israelites—which would take something, given his demeanor and the quite undignified manner of his entrance. (How would you react if he came boiling into your church?) But be careful. This is a clear case of false advertising. The Israelites were being set up and they didn't even see it coming. "Thus says the Sovereign God: for three transgressions of Damascus, and for four, I will not revoke the punishment" (Amos 1:3).

"All right!" chimed the Israelites, always pleased to hear their enemies branded.

"For three transgressions of Gaza, and for four, I will not revoke the punishment." "Huzzah," the crowd chanted.

Amos is really warming to his theme now. "For three transgressions of Tyre, and for four . . ."

"Tell it, brother Amos!"

And so on, clear into chapter 2, as Amos lines out the sins of nations and the rage of God, feeding the enthusiasm of the xenophobic Israelites. Given their privileged rank, who can blame them? It was reassuring to hear that God shared their contempt of the despicable clans on whose obvious social and military inferiority they had so recently capitalized.

Now! Without warning, Amos turned the tables: "For three transgressions of Jacob . . ."

"*Jacob*? Wait a minute. That's getting pretty close to home. True, there's no love lost between us and those morons in the southern kingdom, but all the same, they *are* Jews . . ."

Too late. Like a steel trap, the prophetic fury of God snaps shut on the Israelite's bloated and pompous sensibilities: "Thus says the Sovereign God: For three transgressions of *Israel*, and for four, I will not revoke the punishment" (Amos 2:6, emphasis added).

"How *dare* he? Who does this ignorant lout think he is? What could he possibly be thinking of?"

The covenant, that's what. They may have forgotten the terms of their chosenness, their calling to be God's holy nation, but God had not. And it was precisely this relationship, Amos insisted, that would move God to greater patience with the failings and abuses of Israel's enemies than with Israel's own moral bankruptcy. "You only have I known of all the families of the earth; therefore I will punish you for all your iniquities" (Amos 3:2).

We must pause here briefly to detail the meaning of the verb "to know," as used in God's assertion. In biblical usage, "to know" is not simply to possess some piece of information or to be acquainted with another person. The word is one of those layered concepts that speaks to multiple levels of relationship. And more than one meaning may be implied in a given passage. Knowledge, in scriptural connotation, means not only to be aware *of* another person, but to be acutely aware of the qualities that define my relationship *with* that person.

Among the larger meanings for which Scripture employs "to know" is as a referent to sexual intimacy (see, e.g., Genesis 4:1: "Now the man knew his wife, Eve, and she conceived."). The biblical authors had discerned that for two human beings to have sexual relations is to become aware of each other in a way equalled in no other connection. Further, the experience marks us indelibly. We are changed by it, never to be the same again. We now possess a knowledge of both "self" and "other" that can neither be erased nor forgotten. Once we have known each other, we can never again not know each other.

Among the more glaring inadequacies of current social attitudes toward sexuality is our failure to grasp what seems to have been quite evident to our spiritual forebears three thousand years ago! It is no accident that so pregnant a concept (pun intended) would be employed by the Hebrews to capture the manifold relationship between God and Israel, who "knew" and "were known" in ways not yet apparent to the rest of humanity. It was precisely this that gripped Amos' prophetic mind as he spoke God's own words to an arrogant and errant Israel. The very knowledge that Israel and God shared of each other, the indelible affiliation they shared, made it impossible for God to overlook in Israel what might have been tolerated among a people who were "unknown" and "unknowing."

This image firmly implanted, the prophet spits out a series of bone-chilling couplets, detailing for his audience the irrefutable logic of an angry God. The images (Amos 3:3–8) are all from daily life in the Middle Eastern world: two (read God and Israel) do not talk together unless they have cause; nor does the lion roar, or the snare spring, if there is no kill. The trumpet was the air-raid siren of Amos' time, a clarion that the city was under attack. And then, the dreadful conclusion: "The lion has roared, who will not fear? The Sovereign God has spoken; who can but prophesy?" (3:8).

The book of Amos appears in the Hebrew Scriptures as the third of the minor prophets (the "major" ones are Isaiah, Jeremiah, and Ezekiel; the "minor" prophets complete the Hebrew scriptural canon, from Daniel through Malachi). But though Amos appears eighth on the list, he was, in fact, the earliest of the Hebrew prophets whose words were recorded, preserving for us one of history's most powerful witnesses to moral integrity and social responsibility. This does not mean that Amos was the first "prophet" in Israel. People such as Moses, Elijah, and Samuel enjoy major prophetic status; and there were others, apparently, whose words, for reasons unknown to us, were not recorded. Nor need we assume, simply on the basis of Amos' testy rejection of the title in his own case (see Amos 7:14–15) that he did not embrace his own role as prophet, even if reluctantly. It appears, rather, that Amos was so offended by the corruption of the prophetic profession as a whole that he was unwilling to be identified with it. In fact, the role of prophet was an honored vocation in Israel at the time. A prophet's mantle was often passed from father to son. A prophet was comparable to modern clergy in the sense that they made their living from professional religious work.

An analogous sentiment to that expressed by Amos might be obtained in our own time by substituting "politician" for "prophet." Politics, in spite of what many Americans appear to think, is an honorable profession, and one essential to the conduct of a democracy. The term is derived from the Greek *polis,* meaning "the people," in specific reference to citizenship. Politics is the means by which a representative constitutional government (as opposed to one ruled by a despot) arrives at programs and policies. But when the profession suffers from a general collapse of integrity (or appears to), every politician is deemed "dirty." This sentiment was clearly at work in Amos' mind. So fraudulent was prophetic activity in general, so debased the standing of the prophets under the corrupting effect of political and mercantile excess, that the title itself must be rejected.

Yet Amos could not escape the call to prophesy; his pronouncements, and those of his successors, make crystal clear what it means to be a holy people.

What precisely is prophecy? Easy, someone responds. It is foretelling the future. Wrong. The power to "see into the future" is, more properly, divining or soothsaying. And it usually isn't worth much. A film produced in the 1950s predicting what life would be like in our era is good for a lot of laughs. In the main, however, most soothsayers are never challenged about their predictions because, by the time they are due to take effect, most everyone has lost track of what was said in the first place!

The task of prophecy, on the other hand, is first and foremost to discern the substance of the present moment. Sounds a lot less exciting, doesn't it? In fact, it is much more important, for a simple reason. While secular societies like ours accept the predictions of forecasters as amusing, entertaining, or interesting, we seldom treat them as grounds to change our behavior. We do not, that is, view ourselves as the agents whose actions will bring, or fail to bring, those predictions to reality.

The biblical faith community, on the other hand, was conscious of just that connectedness. They were keenly aware that they were creating their own future. To secure the future as blessing, not curse, required a clear understanding of the moral quality of now. They needed a firm grip on the social, political, economic, and moral forces that were active in their present, as the foundation for a credible prediction of their future.

Why? Because, under the provisions of their covenant, God would hold them accountable for the consequences of their actions. It is for this reason that the words spoken by a true prophet are understood to be God's words, not the prophet's own. A prophetic pronouncement is a divine "state-of-the-union" address—God weighing the nation in the balance, evaluating the degree to which the terms of the covenant are being fulfilled, and stating the consequences.

One final point concerning the difference between biblical prophecy and "predictions of the future" (especially the bald-faced trivia that shouts at us from the front pages of supermarket tabloids): prophecy is never understood to be fatalistic. If today's actions change, so too will tomorrow's outcome. God planned for that, else redemption would be an impossibility!

In consequence, prophecy must always aim at a moving target. The classical prophetic formula is this: Thus says God: (a) because you have done that (your behavior), (b) I will do this (historic consequence), (c) *unless* (here comes the redemptive part) you change your ways, in which case, (d) tomorrow will dawn a blessing, not a curse. It's up to you.

Very well: to the substance of Amos' claim on God's behalf. On this point, Amos joins a small group of biblical voices, a group that includes Isaiah, Micah, and Jesus, in addressing one of theology's oldest conundrums: the relation—and the tension—between ritual adherence and moral action.

The issue troubled the ancient Hebrews, continued to plague the people of Jesus' time, and is unresolved—and likely to remain so—among churches of the late twentieth century. Put most bluntly, the dilemma is this: does right worship or right conduct better serve God?

Some readers may find it helpful to note that the body of statute we call Jewish, or Hebrew Scripture (Old Testament) law, comes in two parts. *Moral* law (of which the Decalogue, or "Ten Commandments," is best-known) guided the personal, social, and business conduct of the nation. From it sprang notions of justice, equity, hospitality, and altruism that have shaped social views in the Western world for several thousand years. *Ritual* law governed the religious life of Israel, with largest attention to two facets: cultic activity, such as holy day observances, the offering of sacrifices, and duties of the priesthood; and matters of purity, such as food choices, health, and bodily functions. Perhaps it was inevitable that two bodies of law addressing such divergent concerns would create confusion and conflict.

It was smack into the middle of this tension that Amos came stomping at Bethel. You see, the people gathered there—Israel's self-anointed 500—came to "worship" the God who was the author of their prosperity. Well, actually, to be blunt about it, they intended to reconfirm their chumminess with the Holy One of history! But here is the problem: even conceding that they fulfilled to the letter the ritual requirements received from Moses, their worship was stained by a fatal flaw: the most extravagant sacrifice imaginable is not sufficient to bribe a righteous God into overlooking a failure of compassion—much less greed, corruption, and injustice. Therein lay the Israelites' ignorance and the ignorance of everyone else who assumes that God can be pacified by "right worship." The very notion that God is pleased by our mouthing some verbal formula while repeating a set of prescribed actions absent the larger moral considerations is to profane worship by reducing it to pretentious magic. It is an attempt to manage God's "mood" and insure divine sanction, not of what we do, but who we are. That, roared Amos, is an engraved invitation to national oblivion.

Worship God? Certainly. We are a people of faith. Fulfill the ancient ritual? Of course. It is a gift from God. But not as a substitute for righteousness! Indeed, forced by human conduct to choose, God angrily brushes aside the ancient ritual—and every liturgy that is its natural issue—to shout the primacy of mercy and justice:

> I hate, I despise your festivals, and I take no delight in your solemn assemblies. Even though you offer me your burnt offerings and grain offerings, I will not accept them; and the offerings of well-being of your fatted animals I will not look upon. Take away from me the noise of your songs; I will not listen to the melody of your harps. But let justice roll down like waters, And righteousness like an ever-flowing stream. (Amos 5:21–24)

It is a theme whose passion and urgency are equalled in only two other places in the Hebrew Scriptures:

In Isaiah 1:11–17:

> What to me is the multitude of your sacrifices? says the Sovereign God; When you come to appear before me, who asked this from your hand? Trample my courts no more; New moon and sabbath and calling of convocation—I cannot endure solemn assemblies [marred] with iniquity, Your new moons and your appointed festivals my soul hates. When you stretch out your hands, I will hide my eyes from you; Even though you make many prayers, I will not listen; [because] your hands are full of blood. Wash yourselves; make yourselves clean; remove the evil of your doings from before my eyes; cease to do evil, learn to do good; seek justice, rescue the oppressed, defend the orphan, plead for the widow.

And Micah 6:6–8:

> "With what shall I come before the Sovereign, and bow myself before God on high? Shall I come before him with burnt offerings, with calves a year old? Will God be pleased with thousands of rams, with ten thousands of rivers of oil? Shall I give my firstborn for my transgression, the fruit of my body for the sin of my soul?" He has showed you, O mortal, what is good; and what does God require of you but to do justice, and to love kindness, and to walk humbly with your God?

It is a compelling theme—and, we need to note, entirely consistent with Jesus' adoption of the proclamation from Isaiah 61:1–2 as the motif of his own gospel mission:

> The Spirit of God is upon me, because God has anointed me, he has sent me to bring good news to the oppressed, to bind up the broken-hearted, to proclaim liberty to the captives, and release to the prisoners; to proclaim the year of God's favor.

In brief, we worship—which is to say we engage in ritual and liturgy—because we are a worshipful people who know ourselves to be loved of God; who know in our flesh the need for divine mercy and the guiding lamp of the Spirit's presence; and who feel compelled to acknowledge that God is sovereign, not us. (Thank God!) But our worship and ritual are not, cannot be, must never become, substitutes for engaging the world's pain with redemptive energy. And more, worship and liturgy must never be a mechanism, as they had become for Amos' Israel, to try to convince God that we are a holy people when God knows different! How serious a mistake this can be is illustrated by the concluding phrase of the passage from Isaiah that Jesus read in the Nazareth synagogue. Luke's account (4:18–19) had Jesus conclude with the words, "to proclaim the year of God's favor." But Isaiah's original (61:2) suggests a God with broader intentions: "and the day of vengeance of our God."

What a wonderful paradox of an image! We are confronted by a holy anger that, in a single gesture, encircles the oppressed with an embrace but falls like a fist on the head of the oppressor. This is not, if you will excuse my parlance, a God to mess with. To be a holy people, we must first be a people of justice. To be a worshipful people, we must first be a people of mercy. To be God's people, we must first be a humble people. There is really no great mystery to it at all. Only a lot of hard work.

The reward is equally clear. Only a holy people are worthy to be the recipients of the ancient, redemptive promise first made to Abram and Sarai, enlarged to embrace their progeny in the Sinai wilderness, and refined in prophetic fire. Thus is the stage set for the day when "every nation of earth will consider itself to have been blessed."

Questions

1. Be honest now: How would you react if Amos came bellowing into your church Sunday morning? How about the rest of your congregation? Who are the Amoses in your congregation? In your town? Is there anyone who, in your judgment, has earned the title "prophet"? How or why?

2. List the things that you see happening in your own community or the nation that you believe portend "blessing or curse" in our own future or the future of

our people. What, if anything, do you conclude might be done either to ensure the blessing or offset the curse. Are you willing to take the necessary steps? Is your congregation?

3. Careful now: Draw up a list the ways in which your congregation balances ritual activity and ethical engagement. Which gets the greater share of attention? Of resources? Are you content with this balance? Had you the authority, how would you change it?

4

Incarnation

If you want a thing done, go—if not, send.

—Benjamin Franklin

Benjamin Franklin certainly had a way with a few words. And while it is doubtful he had incarnation in mind when he penned the adage above, it nevertheless serves our purpose well, highlighting a unique characteristic of divine love as Christians receive it: God did not send Christ to us; God came to us in Christ. I choose to focus on this notion because it is central to understanding something about Christian theology that is unique among the world's great religions.

But a word of warning: to elaborate on its meaning, we must first dispose of an idea that is well established in some parts of the church about what was going on with God-in-Christ. If the common wisdom is to be believed, the story goes something like this: from Creation to the time of Jesus, God tried repeatedly, but in vain, to get human beings to pay attention long enough for the message of salvation to sink in. The Jews, under this scenario, had several opportunities to get that message: through God's intervention to end their slavery in Egypt, by the gift of the law, and finally in the admonitions of the prophets. But they were too thick-headed—in scriptural language, "stiff-necked." Finally, with mounting frustration, God moved to intervene directly in human history in the birth, ministry, death, and resurrection of Jesus. In consequence, all who acknowledge Jesus as Sovereign will be saved and will go to heaven; those who refuse to do so may as well resign themselves: they are going to hell. Especially lost are the Jews because, after all, the Word did become *Jewish* flesh, but even that failed to bring them around. And since they would not listen, the message was redirected to more receptive Gentiles, giving birth to the global church of Jesus Christ.

There are several glaring weaknesses in this account of things, not least of which is that it is born out of, and reinforces, a thinly disguised anti-Semitism that continues to dog and degrade the church. And this a full two millennia after the birth of the One who, we ourselves protest, came into the world to proclaim universal love. Even more flagrant, however, are the theological defects of this view of things.

We have to do here, do we not, with the God whose primary quality is *hesed,* radical faithfulness? It was God who called Abram and Sarai into special relationship and promised that, at the appropriate time, they would see the fulfillment of a majestic promise—that their seed would become a mighty nation. God who reached into Egypt and "with a strong arm" carried the Israelites out of slavery into the wilderness, there to enter with them into a binding covenant that would commit God and people to each other, inseparably and irrevocably, for all time (see, e.g., Exodus 31:16–17). God who through the prophets' testimony reminded Israel of its covenant responsibility as the chosen people of God and urged them to their task. In brief, we are speaking of the God who does not renege on a promise.

Now consider what it must feel like to be a Jew and to be told that the God you have worshiped all your life, who called your forebears to be a holy people, a witness to the nations; who entered with them into a covenant that shaped their personal and corporate life and would continue to do so, "to all their generations," that this God of radical faithfulness has had a change of heart! With such arrogance do Christians glibly set aside four thousand years of sacred history and demean the integrity of the faith community out of which our own originates.

Consider: the Gospels report that Jesus himself said:

> Do not think that I have come to abolish the law or the prophets; I have not come to abolish but to fulfill. For truly I tell you, until heaven and earth pass away, not one letter, not one stroke of a letter, will pass from the law until all is accomplished." (Matthew 5:17–18)

Or, think of his comment to the woman at the Samarian well. "Woman . . . you worship what you do not know; we worship what we know; for salvation comes from the Jews" (John 4:22).

But the most telling incident appears in Mark 12:28–31. Asked which is greatest among the laws of Israel, Jesus quoted two passages: "The first is, 'Hear, O Israel: God is one; you shall love your God with all your heart, with all your soul, with all your mind, and with all your strength.'"

This passage, titled the Shema (pronounced "shmah"), takes its name from the first word of the inscription in Hebrew, which means "hear." Jesus was reciting from Deuteronomy 6:4–5. Indeed, the passage is so basic to Jewish consciousness that it surrounds and permeates every aspect of Jewish life to this day.

"The second," Jesus continued, "is this, 'You shall love your neighbor as yourself,'" a quote from Leviticus 19:18.

Does the choice of these quotations, directly from the body of Jewish law, sound like the choices of one who intended either to downplay, much less to abrogate, Israel's ancient covenant with God? Do these not seem to be the words of one rooted himself in that covenant, who was both respectful of its terms and confident of its viability?

But, someone throws out, Jesus had such obvious disagreements with these people. What about the time he picked up a piece of rope and whipped the money changers out of the temple in Jerusalem, forcefully reminding them that God desired the temple to be a house of prayer for all the nations, but people like them had turned it into a den of robbers (Mark 11:15–17). And wasn't he himself on one occasion asked to leave the neighborhood (Mark 5:16–17), and, on another, thrown out of a synagogue and driven to the edge of town with intent to do him bodily harm (Luke 4:28–30)? What about his lengthy and testy confrontations with the Pharisees (see Matthew 23:13–36)? Is it not clear that Jesus was in fundamental disagreement with many in his own community concerning these issues? Unquestionably!

But let me ask you: do you agree with everyone in the universal church of Jesus Christ in all respects? Universal, did I say? Let me rephrase that: do you even agree with the members of your own congregation all the time? Are you kidding!? Most congregations can't even agree on what color to paint the nursery without someone threatening to walk out the door. I served one church where the debate became so heated that people almost came to blows. Fortunately, they were prevented by an acute attack of embarrassment; and when they sat down to ask one another's forgiveness, they quickly settled on a humorous compromise that remained for years, mute witness to the folly of petty disputation: they painted half the nursery pink and the other half blue.

So Jesus' relations with Jewish leaders were sometimes heated. Does that imply that he intended to abandon his nation or meant for us to despise and ridicule them? Are we forgetting the masses of Jews who followed him, pleading for his compassion? Who brought their sick and suffering to him to be healed—and were? Who asked him to teach them and to explain the law in ways that would help them employ it faithfully, a resource for redemption? How many times do the gospel writers tell us that Jesus "saw the people and had compassion on them"?

Indeed, we can, if we choose, turn the tables. Does Matthew not report (10:5–6) that Jesus instructed his disciples to avoid the Gentiles and to concentrate on the lost children of the house of Israel? And when the Syrophoenician woman begged his aid for her daughter (Mark 7:26–30), he responded curtly (indeed, the words are edged with nastiness) that it is not appropriate to take the children's bread and throw it to dogs.

On balance, the New Testament contains no information to justify the distorted view that Jesus was sent to negate God's covenant with Israel. Much less is there support for anti-Semitic sentiment or action. Such interpretations can be achieved only by distortion. And we do well to take heed: those who accuse God of disloyalty to an eternal promise tread the edge of the abyss. Unless we who are Christian are prepared to entertain the contention that God's mind may yet change in our case by deciding to redefine who Jesus was and what he achieved on our behalf, it ill behooves us to deprecate the tenacity of Jewish commitment to Israel's covenant with a faithful God.

We Christians must come to terms with our feelings on this score, not just for the benefit of Jewish-Christian relations (there are few tragedies on earth more troubling in heaven than animosity between sisters and brothers who are grounded in common spirituality), but for the redemption of the church. Martin Luther King Jr. used to point out that you cannot keep someone down in the gutter without getting down in the mud yourself. Christian anti-Semitism demeans us far more than it does the Jews. And the effort required to maintain it drains essential energy that should be devoted to pursuit of our calling as agents of reconciliation. Worse, it makes a shoddy hypocrisy of claims we make on behalf of God, especially those relating to unconditional love. It so seldom seems to occur to us that non-Christians judge God by our conduct, and the louder we claim to speak for God, the more they are encouraged to do so.

These are complex and troubling issues and will not be resolved here. Nor will I try. But there is another way to approach the whole matter, if we are willing to explore it. It requires only a shift of focus. What happens if we start over again from the beginning? Forget our preoccupation with what the Jews of Jesus' time did or did not do. Ask instead this question: in what sense might Jesus be, for us Gentiles, the fulfillment of God's ancient promise to Abram and Sarai—that through them all the nations of Earth would know themselves to have been blessed? (It will take the rest of this chapter and all of the next to find the answer, so be patient with me.)

To set the stage, a brief story: My first assignment following seminary was on the campus of Syracuse University, where I soon met a young Jewish woman torn by personal and familial issues that had her practically paralyzed. Because her Jewish origin was at the root of her confusion (at least in her mind) she sought out a non-Jew for counseling—me. One day, some weeks into our meetings, she announced, grandly and with conviction, that she was no longer a Jew; she was now a Christian. Never mind niceties like instruction, confession of faith, or baptism. She meant to dispense with such minor hurdles and get right on into it! In demonstration of her "conversion," she joined the choir that sang for Sunday services in the university chapel. In consequence, she was present a few weeks later when a guest clergyman, a giant both corporeally and theologically, delivered a sermon on Psalm 14:1, "Fools say in their hearts, 'there is no God.'"

At a reception following the service, my student—armed with the certitude of the recently converted and fairly breathing fire—marched up to the visiting divine and accosted him steamily: "You are a Christian minister, and you should preach from the New Testament, not the Old." Towering over her, but drawing from some deep well of mingled compassion and firmness, he replied thoughtfully, "Young lady, apparently you have not yet discovered that Christianity is the Gentile's way into Judaism." Despite his evident perceptiveness, I doubt he appreciated just how potent a reply that was to this particular student—or how totally discombobulated she was for the next three weeks!

Would some consider the minister's comment an overstatement? Probably. Would most Christian theologians find it an assertion too tantalizing to ignore? I certainly did. For the core concept behind the remark is sound: that Christianity is the way by which gentiles find themselves drawn into covenant relationship with God, of a kind that first found expression in Israel's response to its national call to servanthood. But with a difference.

Which brings us back to old Ben. His aphorism, printed at the start of this chapter, echoes (or perhaps is echoed by) the old adage, "If you want something done right, do it yourself." Which is precisely what God did. It is the compelling moment in the next unfolding of the ancient promise first announced to Abram and Sarai: "If you want something done, go—if not, send." That God chose to go underlines the point that, for this stage of the job, sending someone else (a Moses or Elijah or Jeremiah) would not do. This step required intimate involvement.

We call it incarnational theology—and it engages us in one of Scripture's most mystifying and disconcerting stories—the birth of Jesus. Does anything in all our normal experience prepare us to confront redemption in swaddling clothes? Oh, sure, we can accept the rise to national prominence of the children of American rural poverty. It is part of our national self-image. "After all," we intone with pious silliness, "anyone can become president." Obviously not everyone can, since we only have one president at a time, and even if none served more than a single term, there could still be at best thirteen presidents during the fifty years of my life expectancy during which I meet the constitutional qualifications for office. But there are, at present count, at least 135 million other Americans who also qualify. Simple arithmetic suggests that 134,999,988 of us won't get elected, no matter how badly we want the job.

Please forgive my seeming cynicism. I offer the assessment above, not to poke fun at American politics, but to make a theological point: as we try to understand what God was doing in Jesus, none of that matters! In coming to us in

Jesus or, to use the Johanine language, when the Word of Creation became human flesh, the object was not to start at the bottom of the ladder in order to demonstrate how honesty and hard work (with maybe some education thrown in) make it possible for us all to climb it successfully. God did not come among us to demonstrate that those born into positions lacking worldly power can acquire a lot of worldly power if they just play their cards right. Nor was Jesus born in a remote Palestinian village in order to demonstrate that (with pluck and the right agent) talent will be recognized and even a peasant kid can become a star of stage and screen, from Jerusalem to Rome.

The fact is that Jesus died in exactly the same estate as he was born. At his birth, his mother had nothing to wrap him in but a piece of swaddling cloth, and he died with nothing left to him but a loin cloth. The wood slats of a feed trough first held him in life and the wood beam of a cross held him last. From beginning to end, in terms of how the world measures these things, Jesus went precisely nowhere.

This thought is hard for some Christians to swallow. If anyone's place in history is secure, we are wont to argue, Jesus is that one. He embodied precisely the qualities that we most admire, that we most covet for ourselves, and, indeed, for the whole human community: if everyone lived like that, what a world it would be! How else to explain the millions who adore him, who try to live as he taught, who make real sacrifices simply to demonstrate the depth of his love and compassion? And yet, measured against the standards of "success" that we routinely affirm, not with what we say but by how we live, Jesus was a failure at virtually everything. He rose through no ranks of professional or commercial achievement. He never married—advantageously or otherwise!—and left no progeny to "carry on his name." He never acquired—indeed he rejected—the marks of social rank or privilege. He never achieved personal worth in the form of monetary wealth or material possession. He was born humbly, lived humbly, died humbly. In what sense, then, was he "successful"?

To come to terms with Jesus we must first be clear about this: nothing that the world has, either to give or withhold, is a useful standard by which to assess the intentions of God. It is not that Jesus was born into the wrong station, or was denied the wealth and power that could have enhanced his social standing, or failed to take advantage of opportunities that life put in his path, yet somehow overcame these flaws and became "successful." It is that these things are extraneous. They simply do not matter.

Well, then, what does? Come with me to the time just before the start of what we call Jesus' public ministry. Responding to whatever urgings of spirit moved him, Jesus walked out to the Jordan River where John the Baptist was at work, there to be baptized. Then, according to Matthew's familiar account (chapter 4), the Spirit led Jesus into the wilderness to be tempted by Satan. Now, anyone familiar with Scripture knows that Satan's intent was to seduce Jesus into abusing his divine powers. If this could be accomplished, Jesus' authority could be corrupted to serve the purposes of evil. Not entirely understood, however, are the dynamics at work in the temptations employed. They are instructive and provide us a parable on the point we are considering.

First, after Jesus had been in the wilderness forty days and nights without food or drink, he was, in one of Scripture's true understatements, famished. Well I guess so! Bread. That's what is needed. Enter Satan, oozing pretentious innocence: why, Jesus, you have power: command these stones to become loaves of bread. Now be clear: the implied intent of this exercise is not to relieve Jesus' appetite, it is to fill the belly of a hungry world. How many news stories have you read or heard in the past five years concerning hunger somewhere in the world? Now imagine you had the ability to turn stones into bread. In no time, people would jump to satisfy your every whim. How long would it take to acquire a million followers? A month? A few weeks? A couple of days? Jesus, urges Satan, ease their physical hunger, and they'll swarm to you!

Next, Jesus finds himself at the pinnacle of the temple in Jerusalem. Jump off, Satan teases. God won't let you be injured. Again, the object is not to call down a demonstration of divine attentiveness, but to sucker a gullible world. The masses do not care about spirituality; they lust after things that divert and entertain. They rush in droves to purchase the latest novelty, no matter how inane, hoping it will deliver some sense of well being. Give them wonders such as they have never seen, and they'll rush to acclaim you. You'll be on every magazine cover and talk show from the Persian Gulf to the Gates of Hercules! Think of the fame that will be yours!

Finally, Jesus is swept up to a mountaintop from which is visible every nation of the world. I can give you all this, Satan hisses. They are starved for strong leaders, someone who will voice their fears and frustrations, give them pride in themselves again, and lead them out to take revenge on their enemies. All you have to do is bow to me, just a teensy bit. A tad of political compromise here, an insignificant lie there, a bit of deceit and graft, that's all it takes. Just think of all the good you can accomplish for such a small price. Why, with my brains and your charisma, we can take over the world!

Do not underestimate the extent of Jesus' vulnerability. To argue that Jesus was, after all, divine and that none of this posed a really serious threat to his security is to miss the point of the narrative. He has been in the wilderness for a long time. He is beyond hungry, he is on his last legs. Personal strength has long since evaporated. There are no physical resources left nor anyone to help him. Oh, we piously intone, God was there. God is always there. Where? What mention does the narrative make of God's immediacy? Or of angelic intervention to strengthen and protect him. There is nothing but silence, a palpable void. No, the whole power of the story demands that we acknowledge this: Jesus was utterly alone.

I cannot let the opportunity pass without drawing to your attention this simple connection: when we recite the prayer that Jesus taught his disciples and pray, "Lead us not into temptation," we aren't talking the hazards of pecan pie during Lent, friends. We aren't even talking a fifty-dollar bill that fell out of someone's purse and lies there with none but old U.S. Grant staring up to see you pick it up. We are talking utter isolation, devoid of resources material or emotional, when we are isolated even from God—and guess who comes traipsing through the door, grinning from here to tomorrow? To be "led into temptation" is to be invited to commit the most self-serving, the most profitable, the most appetite-satiating acts we can imagine, when we have been deprived of every resource on which we normally count to deliver us from the trap.

Except one thing. Listen again to Jesus: "It is written: 'one does not live by bread alone, but by every word that comes from the mouth of God.'"

"It is written: 'Do not put your God to the test.'"

"Away with you Satan, for it is written, 'Worship your God, and serve only God.'"

The moral: when everything else—*everything*—has abandoned us, the Word alone abides and, by it, we will prevail.

Not by power, but the Word. Not by charisma, but the Word. Not by charm and good looks, but the Word. Not by wealth and influence, but the Word. It was this that drove Jesus from the manger to the cross. It was this that caused him to leave life as he entered it, clad in nothing but swaddling cloth. "Naked I came from my mother's womb, and naked I shall return there; God gave, and God has taken away. Blessed be the name of God" (Job 1:21). The value of life, the measure of its achievements, comes always from beyond the world in which life is lived. For gentiles like us, it is deeply symbolic that Jesus' wilderness ordination becomes manifest at the moment he leans on the Word as his sole support—we now call ourselves "Christians" for the same reason: "And the word became flesh and lived among us . . . full of grace and truth" (John 1:14).

So now we are prepared, finally, to answer the question we have been pursuing: what about us Gentiles?

Questions

1. If reading alone, think about what you first learned about the crucifixion of Jesus. If in a group, share your recollections about what you were taught concerning it. To what extent are people in your congregation still concerned to find someone else to blame for the crucifixion of Jesus. To what extent does that thinking include negative images of the Jews? Is the matter addressed? If not, ought it to be?

2. How do we as a society measure success? List, and rank, as honestly as you are able, the qualities or achievements that really impress you when you try to assess someone's life—including your own. Are there any of them you'd like to change? What would you

drop and what would you put in its place? Why don't you? What would you have to do to make such a change?

3. Have you ever been tempted—really tempted? If so, how did it feel? If not, would you like to be? When you really do feel up against it, what resources do you draw on? How might you share them with others who might need them?

5

Death and Resurrection

What you get free costs too much.

—Jean Anouilh

Once again, begin this chapter by not beginning it quite yet. Set it aside, pick up your Bible, and read 2 Corinthians 5:14 through 6:2. Finished? Okay. Now go back and read 5:16–19 a second time with this thought in mind: This passage expresses with exceptional clarity the Christian vision of God's covenant intention in Jesus Christ. It is, indeed, among Christianity's most eloquent explanations of how Christ is the means by which God's ancient promise to Abram and Sarai goes global. In Christ, the final phrase of that promise to Abram and Sarai is fulfilled: that because of them, all the nations of earth would be blessed.

The immediate evidence that the promise is fulfilled is the presence among humanity of the incarnate Word of God, whom we call Jesus the Christ. The steps by which the promise comes to completion, however, bear as much anguish as exultation. This ought not to surprise us. Abram and Sarai's passage to nationhood followed a path brimming with pitfalls and pratfalls. It was anything but a quiet journey! In like manner, the history of the Jewish nation has vacillated between tranquillity and trauma. Why should it be any different during "our" part of the saga? The story of Christianity is not one in which serenity displaces adversity. It is one in which very fallible human beings, Spirit-driven, triumph over adversity in ways that beggar the imagination. Which is hardly surprising; after all, history's leading expert led the way for us.

Let us begin by revisiting two events recorded in Scripture, one in the Hebrew Scriptures and one in the Christian—events that are closely related and are of fundamental importance to an understanding of sacred history. The first event is the Passover/Exodus experience of Israel; the second the Passion of Christ. Each serves as a portal through which a people passes on its way to being transformed from being no people to being God's people; from being just anybody to becoming people of the promise. Each reveals the lengths to which God will go to make a point about divine fidelity. Each defines the ground over which those people will walk "to all their generations."

Review first the history of the Passover—in Hebrew, *Pesach.* The Hebrews have been held in slavery for generations. Even though they must have dreamed of freedom, they dare not hope too openly for emancipation. After all, hope consistently shattered is but a repetitive form of torture. Then, of a sudden, as out of nowhere, comes Moses, saying that the God of their forebears has heard their anguished cries and even now moves to secure their liberation.

But as is often so in times of social upheaval, the dark before the dawn is blackest of all. The more Moses presses for their release, the more sharply on their backs falls the slavemaster's whip. The more they bend toward freedom, the heavier their chains. Inescapably, hope turns to disillusionment, disillusionment to anger, anger to despair. But just when the despair is most palpable, an inexplicable command from God: prepare a feast. A *feast?* What is this, some kind of joke? Well, yes, in a way perhaps it is. For out of desperation's abyss God will command victory—a technique of which this God of ours seems especially fond and one that fills earth and heaven with shouts and laughter.

This is to be no ordinary feast. This is to be the feast of a people prepared, as at the bugle's call, to form up and march. The first ingredient is to be a lamb. Slaughter the lamb and swab the blood on your door posts and lintels—a sign to God to pass over your homes when the angel of death strikes down the firstborn in Egypt, both of people and livestock. Roast the animal whole and devour it before dawn. What you cannot eat, burn. Eat it with *matzoth* (bread baked without yeast—a marching people has no time to lounge about waiting for bread to rise) and bitter herbs (a symbol of your slavery). Eat it standing, with your shoes on your feet, your clothes gathered up for travel, and your staff in your hand. Tomorrow we move!

Oh, and one more thing: "This day shall be a day of remembrance for you. You shall celebrate it as a festival to God; throughout your generations you shall observe it as a perpetual ordinance" (Exodus 12:14).

To fully comprehend *Pesach,* it is essential to remember this: it is observed, not for its own sake, but for where it leads. Had the Israelites left Egypt and wandered off into history someplace, never to be heard from again, Passover would be without meaning, an odd, concluding ritual demarking the boundary between slavery and oblivion. No, Passover is significant because it was the doorway to Sinai where God and Israel pledged themselves to an eternal covenant. And because of that covenant, Israel has observed the Passover of God—and continues to observe it—"through all its generations." It is a feast of historic remembrance; not just of Israel's tortured journey, but of the fulfillment of God's covenant promise to the nation that finds its origin in the seed of Sarai and Abram. With each *Pesach* celebration, Jews recall anew, and teach their children, who they are and whose they are.

Now leap ahead several hundred of those generations. It is evening on the fourteenth day of *Nisan,* the first month of the year according to the Hebrew calendar. On the eve of his crucifixion, Jesus—who alone senses clearly what is coming—gathers his disciples around a table to observe this first day of Passover by keeping the already ancient feast. But on this occasion, it will be different. A world of new beneficiaries are to be added to the rolls of God's chosen. And guess what. Your name is on the invitation list, and so is mine.

Remember the indelicate phrase employed in chapter 1, "cutting a covenant"? Remember how the blood of a sacrificial animal—the seat of its life—was divided and splattered on the consenting parties, sealing the covenant and symbolizing both its gravity and its binding character? On Golgotha it happened again. Only this time, the intent of the covenant was immense in scope: God meant to invite all of humanity into covenental embrace. And only one seal possessed sufficient power and worth to accomplish all that: the blood of God.

This is what Christ was communicating to his disciples (and to us) at the Last Supper. There is profound symbolism in the fact that the formation of the "new" covenant was announced during the very ritual that remembered and reaffirmed the "old" covenant. The timing was neither accident nor coincidence. It was self-conscious and consummately earnest. Jesus intended to drive home the connection between God's fulfillment, at Sinai, of the first part of the promise to Abram and Sarai—that they would become a great nation, a chosen people; and God's fulfillment of the final part of that promise in the passion of Christ—that all nations of earth would know themselves to be blessed. Christ's celebration of *Pesach* with his disciples was a reaffirmation of the "old" covenant that grounded them in Israel's sacred history. His announcement of the "new" covenant, with his own blood as its seal, inaugurated the global phase of the divine promise. At Passover, Jews recite together the time-honored words of the *Haggadah,* the Passover liturgy. By this ritual, they reaffirm their membership in their community of faith: born of divine intervention, shaped by covenant commitment, called to be a holy people.

When Christians reenact the "last supper," we recite together the time-honored words of the Eucharistic liturgy. By this ritual, we reaffirm our membership in the now global community of faith: born of divine intervention, shaped by covenant commitment, called to be a holy people. Just as Israel is commanded to observe Passover "to all their generations," in perpetual remembrance of God's intervention on behalf of the nation, Christians are commanded to break bread and drink wine to all our generations, in perpetual remembrance of God's redemptive gift of self for the sake of the whole world.

You see, the visiting chaplain at Syracuse University wasn't far off after all: by covenant remembrance, Christians really *do* find their way into Judaism.

Before we move on to explore the impact of this "new" covenant on the people of Christ's time and our own, however, we need to sharpen our thinking about the crucifixion of Christ. While we are at it, we again have opportunity to lighten our load a bit by discarding more of the discredited and dog-eared anti-Semitic baggage that the Christian community has been carting around far too long to no good purpose.

It seems to me that we in the churches are guilty of self-contradiction in the way that we react to the death of Christ. On the one hand, we act as if Christ's death were a monumental mistake, one of history's most deplorable miscarriages of justice. If we give credence to the claims of the gospel writers, Christ embodied the closest reach of God's love that humanity has ever experienced—or needs to. As the popular expression goes, it doesn't get any better than this! And yet, when humanity was given the chance to be in intimate contact with this man, who both possessed and personified all that we claim to value, we nailed him to a cross and stood him up to die. The death of so wonderful a person cannot be seen as anything but a tragedy and a travesty. And, driven by visceral emotion, we cry, "Someone oughta hang for this!"

This sentiment, based on a lame reading of Scripture, has prompted Christians to spend twenty centuries and an immense amount of energy, searching for someone to blame. Inevitably—and conveniently—the trail leads to the Jews. Sadly, the major source of this anti-Semitism is our own, uncritical reading of the gospel accounts in which our faith is grounded.

It is a distortion that suffers from two serious flaws. First, if we listen to the whole testimony of early Christians, to accuse the Jews or the Romans or anyone else for the death of

Christ is simply an attempt to shift blame off ourselves, a means to avoid personal responsibility. Granted, this is a theological, not an historic, interpretation. But it is the only one that counts. A central assertion of the passion narratives is that everyone—repeat, *everyone*—turned their back on Christ. To now blame the Jews for whatever details occurred twenty centuries ago is irrelevant. Because we ourselves would have shown no greater loyalty to Jesus than did his own companions—whom we now revere as the founders of the church!

How should we, who find it hard to keep faith with Christ when threatened with little more than the ridicule of skeptics, presume we would have stood by him when a Roman sword was pointed at our throats? Let's admit it: on this score, we ought all to adopt Peter as our patron saint. He denied Christ a mere three times before the rooster crowed. How many of us are prepared to stand before the throne of grace and claim we have done better? Few events challenge us more plainly than to ponder the truth of Jesus' good-natured but biting admonition to his followers: "Why do you see the speck in your neighbor's eye, but do not notice the log in your own eye? You hypocrite! First take the log out of your own eye, and then you will see clearly to take the speck out of your neighbor's eye" (Matthew 7:3, 5). The hard part of that admonition, of course, is figuring out where to stand in order to get a firm hold on that confounded log! One might as well try to pick up a two-by-four while standing on it. Which is why we need God in the first place—not to help us judge others for their lack of virtue, but to come to terms with our own.

Second, Christian faith concedes, indeed professes, that had Christ not died in the manner he did, we would be without hope. Paul puts it starkly: "If for this life only we have hoped in Christ, we are of all people most to be pitied" (1 Corinthians 15:19). If Christ had simply stopped by for a visit and then moved on, leaving behind nothing but a handful of stories and lessons, we would lack one of the compelling fundamentals of New Testament hope: that in Christ, we need no longer be either anxious about life or terrified of death. It is a central tenet of our faith, one of the distinguishing characteristics that sets Christianity apart from other great religions of the world: Christ, the reconciling Word clothed in human flesh, lived and died and was raised again—and on the way by reached out to scoop us up and take us along!

The Good Friday/Easter event trumpets the astounding news that God's love does not evaporate at the lip of the grave; it submits to death on its own terms, transcends it, and drains it of power. The very idea of death is enough to fill many human beings with dread, to drown them in the illusion of despair. In consequence, those preoccupied by death (mainly their own) easily succumb to avarice and greed—"I'll get mine, and the rest of you can go to hell"—failing to realize that they themselves already have. Christians here have the advantage. We know something that humanity before Christ could not know: that the way of death, with all that it represents of futility and despair, and a preoccupation with mortality, which robs us of the courage to live victoriously, do *not* have the last word. In sum, when we are "in Christ," the resurrected One, death no longer has the capacity to dictate the manner of our living. We are able to plunge into life full steam ahead, right into the face of death, because we know that God is sovereign of both life *and* death. Of what shall we any longer be afraid?

But we would never have known all this had Christ not first submitted to death. Absent the resurrection, the cross triumphs; but absent the cross, the very idea of resurrection ceases to have meaning. Christ's death is no less essential to our redemption than is his resurrection. The two are physically and spiritually inseparable, the start-and-finish of the single, climactic moment in God's strategy for "reconciling the world to himself"; not an inexplicable glitch in the plan, but an essential moment in the unfolding of sacred history. For the church, Christ's death, no less than his rising, is a gift to be received in grateful humility. So let us, for Christ's sake (not to mention our own!), stop wallowing in accusations about who is to blame (we *all* are) and get down to some serious celebrating. We who know in our own flesh the power of resurrection are least excused from playing the blame game.

A final consideration: There is a paradox about Christ's death which most Christians seem unaware of or, if aware, have chosen to overlook. Most of us, I suspect, grew up in churches where the crucifixion was mentioned frequently, but in isolation from its cultural framework. In consequence, we tend to think of it as a unique event. Indeed, because we do not *know* its context, most of us have no other way to view it. Oh, we realize, in an abstract kind of way, that the cross was the electric chair of the Roman Empire. I knew that, thanks to a devoted Sunday School teacher, by the time I was in the fifth grade. Perhaps you did too. But in my case (and here I take note of the rich irony permeating this discussion) it took a rabbi to drive the point home. The overriding quality of the crucifixion of Christ, he apprised me, was not that it was unique but that it was so utterly ordinary. Doesn't that, even now, strike you as a contradiction? Doesn't something in you bridle at the very suggestion?

But listen to my friend's illustration. Recalling a deeply troubled time in Jewish history, he related how, in an attempt to break Israel's rebellious spirit and its defiant refusal to bow in submission to the emperor's authority, Roman soldiers crucified several thousand Jews *in a single day.* I found myself stunned by this intelligence, though not for the reason we are conditioned to presume—that it was an atrocity. Of course it was! That surely goes without saying. But the mere mechanical scope of it should not astonish us. The Romans, like Germany under the Nazis, excelled in bureaucratic efficiency, especially in the economy of wholesale massacre. It is an essential requirement of empire. Have I then grown too jaundiced to experience revulsion because of yet another report of yet another atrocity committed in the name of yet another vapid nationalism? I hope not. But I confess that what got my attention was not the rabbi's terrible image. It was its clear—and affirmative—theological significance. I had spent most of my life (my fifth-grade Sunday School teacher's efforts to the contrary notwithstanding) thinking of the crucifixion of Christ as (trumpet fanfare, please) *The Unique Event.* Oh, sure, others died on crosses. But this was *Christ.* Somehow that made it different, imbued it with earth-shaking significance. Well, as a matter of fact it did! But not for the reason I had always assumed.

You see, I had assumed that the death of Christ must be significant because it was somehow different from the death of anyone else ever hung on a cross—or anyone who simply died, period. It was, I imagined, *very* different, simply because it was *his* death. It took a rabbi—one who clearly does not share my view that Christ is "Savior of the world" but who understood far better than I the political and social context in which Christ died—to demonstrate to me that there really was nothing very different about Christ's death after all. The theological power of the event derives not from how Christ's crucifixion differs from all other crucifixions but from its essential similarity. Which is the essential point to be absorbed here: Christ died in precisely the same way that so many other thousands of God's children had already died and would die in the future—many because of their loyalty to him. It was, I suddenly understood, yet another occasion on which God stepped into an abyss of human history and, by participating in it, transformed it. By submitting to that thoroughly unremarkable cross, that most average instrument of pointless suffering, Christ sanctified the pain of everyone who ever suffered or will suffer to nourish the arrogance of despots and tyrants, and threw wide the gates of heaven.

Finally, it was confirmed for me that incarnation truly is a seamless garment. Christ's death on the cross was of a whole piece of cloth with his birth in a stable. As he was given to us by means of the most common of births, he was taken from us by the most common of deaths. Our birth. Our death. This truly was Emmanuel, God with us, in ways that, even now, we do not always fathom. His life parallels the whole of what we each experience as "earthly life"—all the time that we are given, from conception to expiration. He was excused from none of it.

This thought is more important than may at first appear to be the case. Through history, and still today, there are some among us who want terribly to tidy things up by excusing Christ from having to wallow in the whole of what it means to be human, the muck as well as the sunshine. Perhaps we do this to avoid the shame we feel when we look into the mirror. We can endure the stains left on even the best of our souls by lust and envy and greed and dishonesty. But surely Christ faced nothing of that, being divine and all. It won't wash. An incarnation that is less than enveloping is of no value. If God does not take full hold of all that we are and all that we fear and all at which we fail and all to which we aspire, then a part of creation stands unredeemed.

Recall again where this discussion began. Paul does not state that God in Christ was reconciling those parts of the world already judged acceptable, or those parts it pleases us to think acceptable. Paul states that, in Christ, God was reconciling the *world*. No exceptions, no disclaimers, no fear. But then, isn't that precisely what was encompassed by the promise made to Abram and Sarai in the first place? It comes with the territory, don't you see, when we accept an invitation to covenant with a God of radical faithfulness.

Questions

1. What does it mean to claim for ourselves the title of a "covenant people"? What privileges does the title convey? What responsibilities?
2. Were you familiar with the theological connection between Passover and the Last Supper? Between Israel's covenant made at Sinai and the church's covenant made at Golgotha? If you were, how did you come to know? In your judgment, how well are these relationships understood and taught in the churches?
3. What does it mean to you to view the crucifixion of Jesus as "common"? Does it change anything about the way you will think about, and prepare for, Good Friday and Easter? Why?

6

Life in the Spirit

Security is mostly a superstition.
It does not exist in nature. . . . Life is either
a daring adventure or nothing.

—Helen Keller

Helen Keller should know. While yet a tiny child, she suffered neurological damage that left her blind and deaf. Since she could no longer hear, she became largely mute. Regressing to a stage barely equivalent to an animal, she remained trapped in her dark and silent universe for several years until her parents hired a young therapist, herself legally blind, named Ann Sullivan. The story of Sullivan's work with Helen is told in a remarkably moving film called *The Miracle Worker.* Largely through Sullivan's tireless, imaginative, often desperate labor, Helen found her way back into contact with a world, the image and sound of which she could never again know, by training the senses that her affliction left intact—touch, smell, and taste. She began to speak, learned to read, received an education, and, as an adult, went on to write and lecture widely. Helen Keller probably learned as much about security, adventure, and courage as any human being needs to know! And she provides a perfect introduction to Pentecost.

The story of Pentecost is among the most remarkable in Scripture. And it, too, is a story about security, adventure, and courage. The event is often called "the birthday of the church," although it is not always clear what is meant by that expression. If the intention is to designate a date on which the institutional church had its inception, as if it were a matter of administrative bookkeeping, then we've missed the point. If, on the other hand, we intend to point to the gateway through which the apostles passed on their way from being dependent on the physical presence of Jesus to freely assuming responsibility for their own actions in the world, then Pentecost is indeed a birthday, party and all. The difference is not trivial. Assessment of the significance of biblical events must always consider their theological significance, never simply their chronological placement.

The theological significance of Pentecost lies in the "third person of the Trinity," the Holy Spirit, whose engagement in this story is among the most dramatic recorded in Scripture. After the encounter, things would never again be the same for the apostles—or anyone else. But we are getting ahead of ourselves. Unless we absorb what the mood of the apostles must have been in the days preceding Pentecost, we will not appreciate how truly inflammatory this "birthday of the church" really was. Face it: as events began to unfold, this group was anything but dynamic!

Imagine their mood. They took up with Jesus in the first place because he possessed so many appealing qualities: a compelling personality, boundless compassion, the ability to communicate religious wisdom to unsophisticated people—and demonstrable spiritual authority. All of which convinced them, before too much time had passed, that this man was indeed a savior of Israel, perhaps even the promised Messiah. At this point, however, the picture becomes confused. It is unclear just how the disciples thought Jesus would accomplish the anticipated results. No matter. What is clear, by their own confession, is how panicked they were by his arrest, how demoralized by his death, how shocked by his resurrection—the impact of which had to be even more stunning than his death. (We human beings, after all, are far more accustomed to death than resurrection!)

Nonetheless, the ensuing days brought some adjustment—though it was a giddy time to be sure, with their resurrected leader appearing and disappearing and all—sometimes through closed doors! Still, maybe it would all make sense again. Maybe their initial decision to follow Jesus would be vindicated. Maybe the events of recent days had not changed things as much as first appeared to be the case. But then, out of the blue, they learned that the resurrected Christ was leaving again (we call it "Ascension") and did not plan to return until the end of time. So they asked when that might be (under the circumstances a perfectly reasonable question, don't you think?), but he put them off with an enigmatic answer about how it was not for them to have prior knowledge of events set by divine authority and locked away in the mind of God. But not to worry: "You will receive power when the Holy Spirit has come upon you; and you will be my witnesses . . . to the ends of the earth." And then he was gone and that was that.

It was hardly a case of what we now like to call "closure." There they were, absent the One who had focused their lives and activities for three years. He took away their center and left them with nothing but a single instruction and a promise they could not understand (hardly a palliative for what disquieted them). So they did the only thing they knew to do—the thing they had mainly been doing since Jesus' trial and death: they went to their room and hid.

And there they were, still hiding, when the dawn of Pentecost overtook them. Can you not identify with their state of mind, now fifty days after Jesus' death? Dazed, disorganized, demoralized, no longer sure who they were or what they were to do except nothing. But then, that is precisely what Christ instructed them to do. John Milton's poetic phrase may never have been so valid: "They also serve who only stand and wait" (Sonnet XV, "On His Blindness," 1652). And what they discovered next was just what recent events had left them unprepared to expect: they were sitting at the epicenter of a spiritual eruption.

Take a moment here, turn to Acts 2, and read the story for yourself, trying, as you do so, to put yourself in the apostles' place, seeing what they saw, feeling what they felt. Then come back and we will explore a bit of Pentecost's theological significance.

Our word "Pentecost" is Latin, a derivation from the Greek *penta,* meaning "fifty," and denotes the fiftieth day following the second day of Passover. Passover, did I say? Indeed. Once again, Christian meaning is rooted in Jewish history. Jews celebrate Pentecost in the context of *Shabuoth,* the Feast of Weeks, the festival during which the first fruits of each year's harvest are dedicated to God. But Pentecost proper recalls the day on which Israel received the law at Sinai, an event that tradition holds to have occurred fifty days after the Exodus, which began the day after the original Passover. Choice of such dates is never casual. In Jewish faith, the law is a working symbol, Israel's marching orders by which it seeks to live out its covenant responsibility to God. Recall that in the Acts account, it was in observance of this Jewish understanding of Pentecost that "devout Jews from every nation under heaven" had come to Jerusalem (Acts 2:5).

In light of its own Pentecost experience, Christianity adopted a parallel theological interpretation: God's gift of the Holy Spirit is to the Christian church what God's gift of the law is to Israel. As the Jewish Pentecost fell fifty days after day two of Passover, Christian Pentecost fell fifty days after Good Friday—day two of the Passover observance that Jesus shared with his disciples, at which he announced the new covenant. As the law is God's road map for the people of Israel as they seek to remain faithful, through time, to the eternal covenant sealed at Sinai, the Holy Spirit lives in Christian hearts and minds as an indwelling compass, guiding the people as they seek, through time, to remain faithful to the eternal covenant Christ sealed on the cross.

Bear with me as I push this parallel a bit further, if only because we in the church have too long ignored it, depriving ourselves of a clearer understanding of our biblical roots.

A moment ago I referred to "the gift of the law." The expression comes as a surprise to many who, looking into Judaism from outside, think of the law as little more than a bothersome set of rules—antiquated ones at that! Such a view misses the point. Ask any practicing Jew and you will likely be told that the law, far from burdensome, is liberating. The parallel to the Christian understanding of the gift of the Spirit is clear, if we open ourselves to see it: both come as gifts of grace. This is clear enough to Christians, who speak comfortably (perhaps too glibly?) of "the gift of the Holy Spirit." But neither gift was "earned," neither was received because "deserved." Each comes as an act of mercy from a compassionate God who knows, far better than we, how lost we truly are without divine intervention. The mystery is not that these are parallel gifts, but why we should think otherwise. How are we Christians to rationalize the opinion that the same God who showers us with blessings has showered our Jewish neighbors with a meaningless burden? Is this the God of grace that we preach or some other? A strange contradiction indeed.

There is a further parallel, however, that brings us back to our main line of exploration: God included no promise that we will find it easy to live with either gift! God, you see, has this habit of summoning us to become more than we are or believe we can be, sometimes against what seem to be insurmountable odds. This is the lesson of Helen Keller.

For the apostles, too, God had no lightweight trials in mind. Pentecost fulfilled the promise of Christ that they would be baptized in the fire of the Holy Spirit, authenticating their relationship to God and filling them with the courage and zeal necessary to execute their task as ambassadors for Christ to a suffering world. That much was relatively easy. What followed was not. You see, in telling the apostles not to fear the world because he had overcome it, Christ was not claiming that the transformation was complete, only that he'd provided the tools—love and courage and compassion—needed for the remodeling to progress. It was up to the disciples to pick up the tools and get to work. Except that the same evil that hung Christ on the cross was still loose in the world—and not one bit more domesticated! It was not a time when what mattered most was the gain-to-loss ratio of church membership or whether congregational giving would sustain the bottom line. It was a time when simply to confess one's faith could lead to arrest, and refusal to renounce baptismal vows was to invite a death sentence. It would not to be a nice trip.

Indeed, it is amazing that the church survived at all. How many Christians were slaughtered by Roman authorities seeking to stamp out the young church is known only to God. Nor was it the last time in history that obedience to Christ would call forth "the last full measure of devotion."

Reflecting on this, we confront one of the signal mysteries—and central truths—of Christian experience: that the "blood of the martyrs is the seed of the Church" (Tertullian, C.E. 160–240, in *Apologeticus*). The more history's religious and political authorities have lashed out in brutal fury, desperate to stop the spread of this upstart religion, the more numerous the ranks of those who rose up to defy them. It brings to mind the humorous segment in the Walt Disney movie *Fantasia* in which Mickey Mouse is cast as the central character in a cartoon dramatization of Paul Dukas' "The Sorcerer's Apprentice." Fed up with the drudge work required of him and knowing just enough magic to get himself in serious trouble, the cocky apprentice places the wizard's cowl on his own head and commands a broom to fill the cistern. The broom takes up the task with such diligence that the cistern is soon overflowing, at which moment the apprentice belatedly discovers that he does not know how to stop it. Frantic, the apprentice seizes an axe and chops the broom into pieces. But his relief gives way to consternation as each of the resulting splinters rises up and becomes a whole broom and returns to the task of carrying water. With rising desperation, the apprentice struggles to reverse the burgeoning flood, to no avail. Just when chaos seems inevitable, the wizard appears, reestablishes order, and disciplines the errant apprentice.

One can imagine the emperors and officials of Rome—or later persons of self-importance who thought the demolition of the church a worthy political goal—in the place of Mickey

Mouse. Cut down one Christian and ten more rise up. Cut down ten and you face a hundred! How do you stop this menace? Wherein resides a lesson the enemies of the church have not comprehended to this day, though it is well-known to those inflamed by the Guest of Pentecost: as the sorcerer's apprentice could not control the magic, mere mortals are powerless to control the Spirit. Jesus said to Nicodemus: "The wind blows where it chooses, and you hear the sound of it, but you do not know where it comes from or where it is going. So it is with everyone who is born of the Spirit" (John 3:8).

That parallel is not only colorful but theologically valid. The Hebrew word for "spirit" is *ruach,* a term that shares a common root with the words for "wind" and "breath." Would you know where else it appears in Scripture (emphasis added in each instance)? Consider Genesis 1: "In the beginning when God created the heavens and the earth . . . *a wind from God* swept over the face of the water." Or Genesis 2:7: "Then God formed man from the dust of the ground, and *breathed* into his nostrils *the breath of life;* and the man became a living being." Again, "But truly it is the spirit in a mortal, the *breath of the Almighty,* that makes for understanding" (Job 32:7). Or this, from Isaiah 11:4—noting, if you please, that the passage is part of the Messianic prophecies that envision the "shoot out of the stump of Jesse": "He shall strike the earth with the rod of his mouth, and with the breath of his lips he shall kill the wicked." (There is a whole sermon in *that* passage!)

This ingenious image, a product of the Hebrew imagination that found metaphors of the sacred in every aspect of the secular, is useful for those of us struggling to know how the Spirit "works." How do we feel the Spirit's presence? How will we know if and when *we* are visited? Might we not take our first clue from Jesus' observation that God is *always* present? And will we not then be justified, based on the biblical testimony, in concluding that the Spirit is just as constantly with us? In light of this, the images of spirit/wind/breath are especially helpful: think of the Spirit as the air that surrounds and fills you, as embracing as the breeze, as palpable as your breath.

How valid is this metaphor? We need look no farther than Ezekiel's account of his experience in the valley of the dry bones. Part of this prophet's genius was his ability to cast spiritual ideas in images so compelling that, several thousand years later, they continue to influence the vocabulary of everyday life. Few stories fire the imagination like this one—surely among the best known (if less-well understood) of biblical stories. Like few others, this prophecy sets out persuasively the biblical case that human welfare depends absolutely on the presence of divine Spirit. To paraphrase Proverbs, "Where there is no Spirit, the people perish."

The parallels between this story's view of the meaning of "inspiritedness" and what the disciples knew at Pentecost are worth a moment of exploration. So take your Bible again and read Ezekiel 37:1–14.

What commonalities may we suggest between Ezekiel's experience in the valley of the dry bones and the apostle's experience on Pentecost? Before addressing the question directly, we need to do a short piece of interpretive homework. Those who see in Ezekiel's vision of reconnected bones and reconstituted flesh a prophecy concerning bodily resurrection miss the point. Such a view is possible only by a combination of theological revisionism (assuming that Hebrew Scripture exists only to confirm later Christian expectations) and scriptural literalism (that our interpretation of a story is valid *only* if it accepts the face meaning of words). Both assumptions are, in this case, demonstrably false. The central question at issue is, "Can this nation live again?" And the answer is not medical but political and moral. God is not asking Ezekiel to guess whether dead Jews can be resuscitated, but whether there is hope for the nation in the face of its physical destruction and exile at the hands of the Babylonians. Such a hope could be realized only if Israel's moral fire could be rekindled.

That concern aside, what parallels can we now draw? First, note that in both cases, the subjects of God's intentions are hamstrung. Israel, while paralyzed by the destruction of the nation, was first crippled by moral corruption, a betrayal of the covenant that preceded and inaugurated its political collapse. The apostles are hamstrung by the loss of their leader and spend their days in hiding, driven less by faith than by fear. For each, the solution lies outside themselves. Absent the invigorating presence of the Spirit of God, represented by the divine wind, Israel remains nothing but a pile of partially interred bones, the residue of futile combat. Absent the invigorating presence of the Spirit of God, represented by the visitation of the divine wind, the apostles are impotent, life members in the congregation of bystanders. Neither they nor the Gospel is going anywhere.

Second, each event is preceded by a divine promise. God instructs Ezekiel to prophesy to the bones, apprising them that God meant to restore to this people the breath of life, with all its spiritual promise—that is, they would again "know that I am God" (Ezekiel 37:6b). Remember the language of Exodus? "[When] I . . . take you as my people . . . *You shall know that I am your God*" (Exodus 6:7, emphasis added). The nation cannot be restored as a political entity until the covenant is renewed. Christ promises the disciples that, when visited by the Holy Spirit, they would receive power sufficient to drive them to the ends of the earth (Acts 1:8). In the process of discharging their covenant responsibility, they would find both strength and spiritual connection. Both stories remind us that, in scriptural terms, the Spirit's breath is the fount of our vitality both as biological organisms and as moral agents. Absent the Spirit, we are dead; filled with the Spirit, we share that aliveness that is the particular quality of the One-Who-Lives. We are privileged to share nothing less than God's own vitality. Is it any wonder that ten rise up for each one struck down?

Finally, in both stories, the Spirit has a profound impact on all present. Obeying God's command to prophesy, Ezekiel immediately heard a noise, a rattling, as the bones came together. How is this possible, modern sensibility protests. Hearing is a function of the living brain. We all know the litany: airborne vibrations striking the tympanic membrane are communicated to the hearing center of the brain via the auditory nerve, where the signals are processed, analyzed, and interpreted as meaningful sound. Dry skeletons, by definition, lack every single element of such an auditory system. They cannot—to put it bluntly—hear a thing. Yet their bony heads somehow got the message! Does Ezekiel's testimony—even allowing for a nonliteral treatment—strike you as extraordinary, even miraculous? I submit that what happened at Pentecost is every bit as much so. Think of it: a group of Galileans, unlearned folk proficient in a single language—Aramaic—are visited by the Holy Spirit and begin to prophesy. Their words are heard by a large audience consisting of people from "every nation under heaven" who do *not* speak Aramaic; yet the words are understood. Common wisdom holds that the Spirit's intervention constituted an instant short course in foreign language. Suddenly, the disciples weren't speaking Aramaic at all, but all the other languages represented by their audience.

Such an interpretation seems to me narrower than the text allows. It takes into account the assertion of Acts 2:4: "All of them were filled with the Holy Spirit and began to speak in other languages, as the Spirit gave them ability." But it ignores the equally (more?) astounding claim in verse 11: "in our own languages we hear them speaking about God's deeds of power." The parallel with Ezekiel is instructive: the Spirit's first intervention allows Ezekiel to prophesy—with power—to dead bones. By what can only be understood as a concurrent intervention, the bones *understand.* Likewise at Pentecost: we broaden our perception of what happens when the Spirit browses and blows among us if we recognize that such intervention transforms both the mouths of the speakers *and the ears of their audience.*

Christians need again to embrace this truism: never presume that we have a full grip on where the Spirit is going next or the limits of the Spirit's gifts. To do so is to deny two millennia worth of testimony from those who, having been singed by the Spirit's fire, no longer feared the flame. Has anyone ever said it more eloquently that the author of the letter to the Hebrews? "Therefore, since we are surrounded by so great a cloud of witnesses, let us also lay aside every weight and the sin that clings so closely, and let us run with perseverance the race that is set before us, looking to Jesus the pioneer and perfecter of our faith, who for the sake of the joy that was set before him endured the cross, disregarding its shame, and has taken his seat at the right hand of the throne of God" (Hebrews 12:1–2).

Questions

1. Take a few minutes to try—really try—to imagine yourself in the place of Helen Keller. How do you feel? What does it do to your perception about the "fairness of life"? What would you do in her circumstances?

2. Consider what is meant by "the gifts of the Spirit." Make a list of everything you can think of that seems to you to represent the presence of the Spirit of God among the community of faith. How broadly are you willing to define this presence?

3. It is Pentecost day, but your congregation stands in the place of the apostles. A holy wind begins to blow through the house and tongues of fire appear over each of your heads. (Don't argue with me. You're really not so different from the disciples, you know.) Now, what is the Spirit asking of you? Are you ready to give it?

7

Life in the Church

Christianity might be a good thing if anyone ever tried it.

—George Bernard Shaw

The brief discussion of the apostles in the last chapter concludes the review of sacred history—or so common wisdom would have us believe. Well, no, in fact, we have not finished. It has only just begun. Unless, that is, we accept the view that has tended to dominate Christian self-understanding for centuries: that divine revelation essentially ended with the closing of the canon. What do these words mean—the closing of the canon?

Here we go again on a brief digression.

The Interpreter's Dictionary of the Bible defines "canon" as "the collection of early Christian writings venerated as sacred scripture by the church, read in the liturgy, and recognized as the authoritative expression of the apostolic faith."

Recall that the early church's *original* Scriptures consisted of what we now call the Hebrew Scriptures or Old Testament—the collected writings of historic Judaism which Jesus himself honored as a true (if not final) revelation of God. As Christianity took root, however, first in the Jewish community, then across the Greco-Roman world, bits and pieces of new writings began to emerge—letters, essays, accounts of events—which their holders also claimed were "sacred." Inevitably, arguments sprang up and Christian congregations were split by conflicting ideas. To avoid total anarchy, a decision had to be made about which writings would be deemed authentic and which counterfeit.

To explain the process by which this occurred would teach most readers more about canonical development than they care to know. Suffice it to say that the specific collection of writings that we now call the Bible had largely taken shape by the beginning of the third century of the current era. But whence this adjective, "canonical"? Why do students of the Bible refer to Scripture as "the canon"? The term originated in Arabic and Hebrew languages, but came to us via the Greek *kanna* or *kanne,* meaning "reed" or hollow tube. From this we derive three uses, all hinting at some degree of enforcement: "cane" (not as in "to lean on" but "to whip with"), "cannon" (need I elaborate?), and "canon," or "rule," in the sense of a carpenter's tape measure. Thus, "canon" refers to a rule, law, or standard. When we speak of the New Testament as canonical, therefore, we mean that it is the authoritative standard by which all things of the faith are weighed and evaluated. As you process this thought, bear in mind that the very existence of a canon implies the existence of a *non*-canon. Dozens of early Christian writings were not included in our Bible, including several "gospels," some possessing useful insight and spiritual value.

(Contemporary scholars are revisiting these writings with renewed interest, often yielding fresh information about the faith of the early church.)

That the church needed to undertake this task goes without saying. The evangelical mission of early Christians was tough enough without constantly being sidetracked into debates about who had the story right. Unfortunately, the decision to "close the canon" had a corollary consequence that, I suspect, was neither intended nor foreseen: the closing of people's minds to the possibility that God's revelation might just be ongoing. It was as if putting covers on both ends of the text unwittingly put blinders on the people of God! Have you not felt it? Doesn't a lot of preaching and teaching convince you, even though few may come right out and say so, that divine self-disclosure stopped about the time John put the period after the final "Amen" in Revelation 22? Aren't we persuaded that the *real* spiritual story ended two thousand years ago, as if God closed the book and went on extended vacation to Palm Beach? Oh, sure, we have to deal with important religious concerns; but these aren't revelation, they're only the latest consequences of what happened back then. The feature film is over, and all that's left for us newcomers is to help roll the credits.

Is it any wonder that so many Christians are discouraged? Or that non-Christians avoid us because we seem more than anything to be adherents of an ancient and moribund philosophy with little of relevance to offer people struggling to make it in the late twentieth century? If the author of Ecclesiastes is right, that "What has been is what will be, and what has been done is what will be done; there is nothing new under the sun" (1:9), then we Christians really *are* out of it.

Don't count on it.

Be very clear about what the issue is here. For Christians, it is never whether God is active, but whether we are paying attention. If revelation has stopped, the fault does not lie with the closing of the canon but with our failure to hear God's voice in the events of our time, as our forebears in faith heard it in theirs. Unable to see the holy in common things, indifferent to our calling as a covenant people, shamed by the cross of Christ, afraid of the Spirit's flame, we fail to recognize that we, too, have authorized standing in the historic train of God's witnesses; that we are, for our generation, living evidence of God's presence and action. Called to live as children of light, we mistakenly believe that the originating Light went out of the universe long before we came on the scene; we have only the afterglow to guide us and are ourselves no more than a dim reflection of revelation's former glory.

It doesn't have to be this way. That is the whole point of this Lenten exercise: to rediscover the biblical truth that God is *always* present, *always* active among us. The only barriers that hinder us are the ones we erect ourselves.

What can we do about this? The answer, I suggest, is communion—not simply eucharistic celebration (though that is central to Christian life) but broadly defined as the way we live, the frame of reference for all that we do, the posture we assume toward the world. Since Scripture has served as a productive point of departure for these essays thus far, it certainly wouldn't hurt to turn there again! So take your Bible and read Romans 12, in which the Apostle Paul provides a concise outline of daily Christian conduct. Take time to review it thoughtfully, asking yourself how well you embody each of the habits Paul recommends.

"But wait," someone protests. "This is just a laundry list. Where's the inspiration, the insight, the spiritual awakening we need to become alert to revelation?" It is a fair question—but the very asking of it supports the main point we are considering. The fact is, contemporary Christians often look for the wrong end of the answer first. Conditioned by the methods of our scientific/technological age, we assume that we must first identify some intellectual principle or theological insight, a set of intelligible instructions, as a precondition to figuring out what we are supposed to do. I argue the contrary: most of us know perfectly well what it is we are supposed to do; we've either forgotten—or never learned—that in Christian life, reflection follows action, not *vice versa.* Intellectualizing is often simply an excuse for inaction.

The participants in an international youth gathering, students from nations all over the globe, spent their first morning together engaged in Bible study. After all, they were Christians and Christians always begin with Scripture, right? As the session progressed, however, they grew increasingly restless and those who planned the event realized that their program was going nowhere fast. Taking a break, the leaders went to the manager of the camp at which they were gathered and asked if there was a job the group could do, some project to help the camp. The offer reflected as much of desperation as insight, but no matter. They didn't have to ask twice. Rounding up a load of tools, the manager soon had the entire group in mud up to its ankles, digging a drainage ditch. The process of getting started was itself a bit of a challenge: some of the students came from nations where, by social custom, the educated do not work with their hands. Their task is intellectual. Indeed, manual labor is considered demeaning, an embarrassment and a disgrace. Their reluctance to take up picks, shovels, and hoes and address the work was met by a simple but effective assertion: "Christians work together, no matter the task." (It *does* have biblical precedent!)

The ditch completed, the students scraped off the accumulated filth, showered, had lunch, and returned to their Bible study. Immediately, there was a startling transformation. The afternoon session took off, ideas flooding the room as the participants, no longer strangers because bonded by their labor, employed a dozen cultural lenses to share and acquire new insight into their common faith.

Millard Fuller, co-founder of Habitat for Humanity, tells a story that is a variation on the same theme. Christians, Fuller notes, disagree about many things. We argue about Scripture, contend over theology. We cannot agree on doctrine or church governance. And as far as baptism is concerned, we can't even agree on how to get wet! The list of what divides us is vastly longer than what unites us. But on at least this one point, Fuller urges, Christians agree: that at the end of the day, everyone in the world ought to be able to come home to a simple, decent house. Noteworthy by its absence from Fuller's appraisal is any suggestion that Christians have to resolve their theological disputes before they can tackle housing for the poor. To the contrary, Fuller shows how quickly a concerted pursuit of mercy makes mincemeat of theological division. Two ministers signed up for the same building project, one a flannel-mouthed liberal, the other a red-neck conservative. They wanted nothing to do with each other—so the project leaders put them up on the roof together where they spent an entire day laying shingles. At day's end, Fuller reports, they came down off the roof fast friends—and it was a profound embarrassment to both of them!

What those two ministers discovered was that God, to whom each lay claim according to personal definitions, escaped—laughing all the way—from the constraints they sought to impose and caught them both up in a relationship neither anticipated or wanted. And both, to their amazement, found themselves liberated by the experience.

Somewhere along the line, you see, we lose sight of one of the New Testament's most astounding claims: that *each of us is a revelation of God to someone else.* Christian responsibility seldom strikes home more forcefully than when we realize that others judge God's faithfulness and mercy, not by our theological abstractions, but our actions. A young mother participating in a family retreat I conducted could not have said it better. We were exploring the expectations wives and husbands have of each other when she voiced a sentiment quickly seconded by the others in the group: "Talk is cheap. It's performance that counts!" Martin Luther spoke of it as "the priesthood of all believers," admonishing all Christians to be, each one of us, "Christ to our neighbor."

"But how?" our resident skeptics inquire. "How do we do this? How do we *demonstrate* it?" Isn't it odd that we should even have to ask the question? And doesn't it tell a lot about how little we understand ourselves to be agents of God's ongoing revelation?

Through the seven chapters of this book we have been telling stories. Why these particular stories? Because our faith teaches that they are the stories of those who have modeled before the world, in their time, what it means to be the people of God. And now it is our turn. Each of us, don't you see, not only has a story, each of us *is* a story—an account related not just by what we believe but through what we do. Is this so surprising? Abraham and Sarah, Moses, Amos, Jesus, the apostles—each had a story, the aggregate of which makes up the sacred history on which this Lenten study has focused—the sacred history with which we seek to be identified as persons and as congregations. If we want to know how we contribute to sacred history, how we add our own footprint to it, we need look no further than our stories.

How about this one? Some years ago, a young man from Erie, Pennsylvania, traveled to Haiti on a senior-high fellowship service project mounted by his home church. The group spent several days doing repair work at the medical clinic of a mission station. As is the case with most such facilities in rural Haiti, the clinic stood in the center of abject poverty, devoid of resources. Almost.

At noon one day, Dale wandered off down to the bank of a nearby river and climbed atop a large rock to eat his lunch—a single, rather spare sandwich with which to quell a burgeoning appetite that the passing days were doing nothing to diminish. Sandwich poised a few centimeters in front of his face, mouth agape in ravenous anticipation, he suddenly had the feeling he wasn't alone. Glancing about, he found himself looking directly into the face of a small Haitian boy, perhaps six years old, whose large, dark eyes considered him dispassionately. There was not even a hint of emotion. Dale had not previously seen the child around the clinic and had no idea where he came from. But he knew enough of Haiti to know that the child never had enough to eat.

The boy said not a word, just stood there, a few feet away, watching Dale. Dale looked at the boy, then at his sandwich, then back at the boy. Then, shame quelling his appetite in ways food never could have, he grumbled to himself, "Oh, what the heck!" and held the sandwich out to the boy. The child took the sandwich, still without a word, still with no display of emotion. But, to Dale's surprise, he did not bite into it. Instead, he climbed up on the rock and settled down beside Dale, carefully tore the sandwich into halves, and gave one back to Dale. And there they sat, a stunned American teenager and a tiny Haitian boy, side by side on a rock by a river, sharing lunch.

I challenge you to more perfectly describe the essence of communion.

The beauty of this image, don't you see, is that anyone can do it. We are all, everyone of us, avenues of grace. Anyone can be part of the story of redemption. No exceptional skills, no professional training, no special tools are required. Only a loving heart and open spirit. And it is more common than we generally acknowledge. My own introduction to it came in a totally unexpected encounter—one that I tried very hard at first to avoid! Five years out of seminary, while attending graduate school, I was putting food on the table by working as director of education at an urban church. Early one morning, the father of a girl in my youth fellowship group, a professor at the university, fell over dead while standing in his own bathroom shaving, the victim of a sudden and massive heart attack. There was absolutely no warning. The shock waves of his collapse reverberated across the city, through both church and university homes.

As the news spread, members of the youth group came to me saying they wanted to purchase several hymnals as a memorial—would it be appropriate to do so? I suggested we ask the family and called their home. The phone was answered by a woman also connected to both the university and the church. But when I explained the reason for my call and asked her to convey the request to the newly widowed Mary, she called my bluff: "I think you should ask her yourself."

"Well, Ann," I stammered a bit stupidly, "I've been staying away because I didn't want to complicate things for the family."

"I think," Ann responded gently but very pointedly, "that she would really like to see *you*." Something about the way she said it put me on notice that she wasn't telling me all she knew.

Next day, feeling more than a little dread, I approached Mary's door and rang the bell. Actually, you see, I had lied the previous day. I hadn't gone before because I was scared out of my wits. Seminary trains you for many things but calling on a family that just lost a loved one is not among them. At that moment I was engaged in full-bore on-the-job training and there was no way for me but to blunder my way through it as best I could and trust to the mercy of God. Would I were that smart!

The door was answered by Mary's sister, who asked me to wait in the living room: Mary was eating for the first time since her husband died. A moment later, a drained, puffy-eyed Mary, clad in slippers and housecoat, hair looking as if she'd just been caught in a hurricane, swept into the room, both arms extended and hands wide to receive mine, and saying, "Oh, you don't know how happy you've made me by coming!"

And there I was with my face hanging out. I'd come to her house thinking that it was my task to bring some comfort, some touch of assurance, to this woman who had, a mere 36 hours before, lost the love of her life without the slightest chance to say goodbye. I came anxiously, untrusting, preoccupied with my self-image, chagrined that it was so fragile. And out of the depth of her faith and goodness, this tragically torn woman reached out and handed me a silver platter full of grace.

Trust me: I shall remember Mary with gratitude and affection until my dying day.

In such ways do we allow uncertain egos to erect defenses against the inpouring of the Holy Spirit. Perhaps we cannot help it. Maybe it is simply evidence (as if we needed any more) of the fallibility that defines us. Perhaps we are doomed to go on blundering our way through, doing the best we can, knowing it is far from perfect, trusting to God to redeem the effort. But there is another side to these stories, one that enriches them in ways we are unable to anticipate—especially when we are absorbed in playing "O you of little faith": *sometimes God turns the tables on us.* The poor minister to the rich, the hungry to the well-fed, the sick to the healthy, the grieving to the comforters, the dying to their mourners.

It is an insight that, taken seriously, cannot help but broaden our view of who comprises the church. If any and all may, at any moment in time, be both recipients *and* ministers of God's mercy, then who may not be part of sacred history? If our stories manifest the Spirit's burning in every family of the wondrous diversity that is humanity, who may not be my sister and brother in Christ? The scope of who it is that God means to invite to the feast, you see, is not ours to define. We are not put in charge of the guest list. But we err doubly if with one breath we make this confession and with the next continue to assert that we have the ability to look around and discern who has or has not responded correctly to the invitation. It's not always clear who else received one!

A young Lutheran pastor called to a parish on the edge of Harlem was frustrated, after the passage of some weeks, by the nagging realization that he was achieving nothing. Little of anything seemed to be happening in the life of the parish. One day he called on the organist—a woman who had, he opined, served the church at least since the ark had settled atop Mt. Ararat. She heard him out, then asked, "Did you come here believing that it was your job to bring Christ to Harlem?"

"Well, yes," he replied. "That was my understanding."

Her next question caught him totally off guard: "What made you think he wasn't already here?"

This young pastor's experience was a peculiarly American one. It is not by accident that so many American Christian groups stress "personal salvation" or "a personal relationship with Christ." Nor, sadly, is the idea very biblical. These concepts are rooted less in Scripture than in the American mythology of "rugged individualism," the belief that "we are all in this alone." Rugged individualism holds that one person, by dint of grit and ingenuity, can wrest success from the savage wilderness. It is a deeply flawed concept. European immigrants succeeded in forging a new life on the American continent by nurturing social cohesiveness, not willful separateness. The rugged individual is a figment of overactive imagination, much of it in the entertainment industry. So with Christians. Christ does not call us principally into personal relationship, but community; not to passive personal salvation, but to active engagement in the struggle for justice and peace. From a scriptural viewpoint, preoccupation with personal salvation is at best irrelevant, at worst counterproductive. "For those who want to save their life will lose it, and those who lose their life for my sake will find it" (Matthew 16:25).

In a July 4, 1996, editorial, Joan Clifford Hutter, editor of *The Chautauquan Daily,* the summer newspaper of Chautauqua Institution in southwestern New York State, wove the twin perceptions of universality and mutuality into the fabric of what we like to believe is our national community, but with a hauntingly Christian twist:

> Our lives are parables for each other. I observe yours; you gaze through the windows of mine. May we grow more transparent and less guarded; may we walk in the light of honesty, that we may learn and discover the stories, lives and messages, the varied definitions of the liberty exhibited in our individuality.
>
> Isn't that a form of communion? We graze through our days, feed on hopes and dreams, memory and idea; we experience one another's lives; we are broken bread and poured out wine for one another. Walls crumble. Perception widens. And we, like desert tributaries, flow together in the confluence of time and space and being.

Well, we've come to the end. In good evangelical fashion, we ought to close with an altar call! That is not as humorous as we often make it out to be. In sacred history, decision is everything. I match my footprints to those who went before me only when I will myself to walk the road they walked, with all that that implies of hope and challenge, sacrifice and rebirth.

Lent is the Christian's season to decide. Are you ready?

At this conclusion, instead of posing and answering questions, try something different. Stringfellow Barr once commented that Christians, when they get together, have three legitimate tasks: to worship, to study, and to plot. Were you not part of a worshiping community, you probably wouldn't be reading this book, so I assume you worship. For the past seven weeks, you have presumably been using this book as a resource, so I assume you have studied, alone or in a group.

Now, an assignment in sacred plotting: make a list of tasks to which you are prepared to commit yourself between now and the start of Advent, with two goals: to demonstrate as clearly as you can that you are a living agent of sacred history and to demonstrate to someone else, in a palpable way, that God's mercy is at work in you for their benefit.

Shalom.